Cover: Barred gates prevent relatives of freed hostages getting into Hospital No. 13, where dozens of hostages were treated for the effects of fentanyl gas and other injuries after the Moscow theatre hostage crisis in October 2002.
© AP/Sergei Grits

Amnesty International is a worldwide movement of people who campaign for internationally recognized human rights.

Amnesty International's vision is of a world in which every person enjoys all of the human rights enshrined in the Universal Declaration of Human Rights and other international human rights standards.

In pursuit of this vision, Amnesty International's mission is to undertake research and action focused on preventing and ending grave abuses of the rights to physical and mental integrity, freedom of conscience and expression, and freedom from discrimination, within the context of its work to promote all human rights.

Amnesty International is independent of any government, political ideology, economic interest or religion. It does not support or oppose any government or political system, nor does it support or oppose the views of the victims whose rights it seeks to protect. It is concerned solely with the impartial protection of human rights.

Amnesty International has a varied network of members and supporters around the world. At the latest count, there were more than 1.5 million members, supporters and subscribers in over 150 countries and territories in every region of the world. Although they come from many different backgrounds and have widely different political and religious beliefs, they are united by a determination to work for a world where everyone enjoys human rights.

Amnesty International is a democratic, self-governing movement. Major policy decisions are taken by an International Council made up of representatives from all national sections.

Amnesty International's national sections and local volunteer groups are primarily responsible for funding the movement. No funds are sought or accepted from governments for Amnesty International's work investigating and campaigning against human rights violations.

ROUGH JUSTICE:
The law and human rights in the Russian Federation

Amnesty International Publications

Please note that readers may find some of the photographs and case histories contained in this report disturbing.

First published in 2003 by
Amnesty International Publications
International Secretariat
Peter Benenson House
1 Easton Street
London WC1X 0DW
United Kingdom

http://www.amnesty.org/russia

© Copyright
Amnesty International Publications 2003
ISBN: 0-86210-338-X
AI Index: EUR 46/054/2003
Original language: English

Printed by:
The Alden Press
Osney Mead
Oxford
United Kingdom

CONTENTS

Glossary

Convention against Torture	UN Convention against Torture and Other Cruel, Inhuman or Degrading Treatment or Punishment
CPC	Criminal Procedure Code (*Ugolovno protsessualnyi kodeks*)
CPT	European Committee for the Prevention of Torture and Inhuman or Degrading Treatment or Punishment
ECHR	European Convention for the Protection of Human Rights and Fundamental Freedoms
ICCPR	International Covenant on Civil and Political Rights
internat	orphanage
OMON	*Otriad militsii osobogo naznacheniia* (special police detachments or riot police)
OSCE	Organization for Security and Co-operation in Europe
procuracy	The official state body responsible for conducting criminal prosecutions
propiska	system of registration
State *Duma*	Federal parliament
RSFSR	Russian Soviet Federative Socialist Republic (1918-1991)
USSR	Union of Soviet Socialist Republics, or Soviet Union, dissolved in 1991

Chapter 1: Introduction

The Russian Federation's transition towards a market economy from one based on "administrative commands" has been visible to anyone visiting the country since it became a sovereign state in December 1991. Less visible has been the tortuous change to its system of justice. This began in August 1991, when Boris Yeltsin — then President of the Russian Soviet Federative Socialist Republic (RSFSR) — banned Communist Party organizations in the courts and all other workplaces.

This report, written in April 2003 — some 12 years since the Russian Federation began to make fundamental changes to its system of government — focuses on the legal changes. Through information drawn from more than 20 regions, much collected firsthand on research visits and during trial observations, the report examines how far the reforms made so far have given people a quick, fair and effective remedy when they have been wronged.[1]

Two wars in the Chechen Republic (Chechnya) have blackened the Russian Federation's first years as a sovereign state, with gross abuses of human rights committed by government forces and Chechen fighters. Government forces have so far been prosecuted for these crimes in very few cases, and then after long delays. The wars have also highlighted the institutional flaws that impede people's full enjoyment of their human rights in the 88 other constituent parts (Subjects) of the world's largest state.[2] Some groups — such as children born with mental disability and prisoners — are particularly vulnerable to abuses of their rights.

Almost none of the institutions described in this report exist in Chechnya. People living there have no clemency commission, no regional parliamentary ombudsman and, between late 1999 and late 2001, they had no courts. Reforms under the new Criminal Procedure Code (CPC) will not reach them before 2007.

The authorities in the Russian Federation are obliged to ensure that everyone has effective protection against violations of their human rights. In light of the country's recent human rights record, it is particularly important that people are protected from torture, unfair trials, the death penalty, unlawful killings, arbitrary detention and discrimination, and that everyone has access to effective remedies if their rights are violated. It is also important that no one should be returned to a country where they would be at risk of torture, execution or unfair trial.

The Soviet legacy

The legacy of the Union of Soviet Socialist Republics (USSR) has placed massive obstacles in the way of the Russian Federation's self-declared goal of becoming a society based on the rule of law. One of these is the insignificant role that courts played in the past.

The Bolsheviks came to power in 1917 intent upon abolishing law and the courts altogether. They modified their position when it became clear that a state without law deprives itself of legitimacy. What evolved in the USSR was an "administered society". The power to resolve disputes lay not with the courts but with Communist Party and government functionaries. In this context, the courts posed no independent challenge to the ruling system and were little more than appendages to it.

Close to its point of collapse in 1991, the USSR had a population of 260 million people, but only 15,781 judges.[3] This was approximately the same number as in what was then the Federal Republic of Germany, a country with a quarter of the USSR's population. Soviet judges were reputedly the least qualified of the nation's jurists. Membership of the Communist Party was obligatory for judges, and the Ministry of Justice – an arm of the executive – controlled allocation of resources in a way perceived as open to political pressure and thereby undermining independence. Until 1989 the promotion of judges depended on the recommendation of Communist Party officials. From 1989 to 1991 the power to appoint and promote judges was transferred to members of the parliament – the Congress of Soviet People's Deputies – but judges were still not independent. Always predominantly female, the profession became mostly young and inexperienced after the economic deterioration of the mid-1980s left many judges too poor to stay in their job.

The status of Soviet judges was so low that they commanded virtually no respect. Professionally, they played what has been

Relatives of missing people near the office of the President's Special Representative on Human Rights and Freedoms in Chechnya, at Znamenskoe, in 2000. Although foreign observers have sometimes described the Representative as an "ombudsman", he is in fact part of the Russian Federation government and has no independent investigatory powers.

described as a "supporting role" in the system of Soviet justice. The state prosecution service — the procuracy — was the body officially charged with ensuring that the law was respected in every area of Soviet life, even to the extent of "protesting" court decisions it disagreed with. Because administrative solutions were preferred in the USSR, the range of issues that came before the courts was limited compared with courts in many other countries. The incestuous relationship between judges and the Communist Party meant that judges were required to attend party meetings at their place of work, to implement directives from the party apparatus and to place political loyalty above the law. Courts were mobilized behind "law and order" campaigns and willingly complied with official campaigns to obliterate dissent. All this was monitored and documented by Amnesty International.[4]

At the time of its collapse, the USSR was party to several UN treaties on human rights, most notably the International Covenant on Civil and Political Rights (ICCPR) and the International Covenant on Economic, Social and Cultural Rights — both of which came into force in the country in 1976. When the authorities ratified the (first) Optional Protocol to the ICCPR in

1991, they authorized the (UN) Human Rights Committee to examine complaints against them from individuals who felt that their rights under the ICCPR had been violated. In 1987 the USSR had recognized the competence of the Committee against Torture to receive individual complaints against it after it ratified the (UN) Convention against Torture and Other Cruel, Inhuman or Degrading Treatment or Punishment (Convention against Torture).

During its 73-year history the USSR had four Constitutions, but no constitutional court to interpret them.[5] In 1989 a Committee for Constitutional Supervision was set up. Although the Committee lacked the competence of a court, it made several bold rulings that reflected the mood for legal reform being voiced in the country at the time. Most notably, it ruled that the state must publish all laws and regulations, or abolish them, and that the *propiska* (the system for registering residency) was unconstitutional. To this day, this system of registration hinders freedom of movement and residence in parts of the Russian Federation; **Chapter 4** describes the current Constitutional Court's battle to end it.[6]

Emergence of courts

At its birth in 1991, the Russian Federation publicly committed itself to being a state based on the rule of law, with respect for the human rights of its citizens as its main priority. Article 2 of the 1993 Constitution states:

> *"The individual and the individual's rights and freedoms represent the highest value. It is the duty of the state to recognize, respect and protect the rights and freedoms of the individual and the citizen."*

Since 1991 there has been a constant battle between these aspirations and political expediency – often accompanied by the use of force. Part of the struggle has revolved around the emergence of parliament (the State *Duma*) as an independent power.[7] Part has revolved around the role of the courts and their power to dispense justice. This struggle continues.

Two landmarks have been reached, both concerning courts. In 1991 the Russian Federation established a Constitutional

Aleksandr Nikitin, an ecologist, was arrested in 1995 on a false espionage charge: Amnesty International considered him to be a prisoner of conscience. Despite years deprived of his liberty in investigative detention and many changes to the accusations against him, the authorities were unable to secure his conviction. His case was sent back for further investigation 13 times while he remained in prison. After the April 1999 Constitutional Court ruling (see page 6), the St Petersburg City Court immediately acquitted Aleksandr Nikitin and ordered his release. The decision was upheld by the Supreme Court against a protest by the procuracy. Despite a complicated political setting, the judiciary exercised independence, consistency and respect for the law. The picture shows him with his two lawyers and holding the report for which he was arrested; the report accuses the Russian Federation of dumping nuclear waste in the Sea of Japan.

Court to interpret and enforce the Constitution.[8] Among its functions, the Court can hear complaints from individuals who believe their constitutional rights have been violated by the way in which an existing law has been implemented. This has led the Court to make decisions in the field of human rights on numerous occasions. The second landmark was a ruling by the Constitutional Court in February 1999 that the death penalty was unconstitutional until it could be applied equally throughout the federation in jury trials. This led to an effective moratorium on capital punishment.[9]

© Heidi Bradner/Panos Pictures

The Russian Federation's international treaty obligations form an integral part of its domestic law, and must prevail in cases where the two diverge.[10] Since 1991 the Constitutional Court has passed rulings in light of this principle and raised the standards required of national bodies, especially in the field of criminal procedure.[11] In April 1999, for instance, it ruled that when courts cannot convict an accused, they must immediately acquit.[12] This ended the traditional practice of sending cases back for "reinvestigation" until the prosecution was able to get the judgment it desired.

When it became a sovereign state, the Russian Federation assumed all the international treaty obligations of the USSR. In 1998 it also ratified the European Convention for the Protection of Human Rights and Fundamental Freedoms (known as the European Convention on Human Rights — ECHR), recognizing the right of individuals to bring complaints against it to the European Court of Human Rights, and promising to be bound by the Court's rulings.[13] At the time of preparing this report, the European Court of Human Rights had passed judgment in the first cases brought against the

Lydia Andreevna, from Novo-Cheboksary in the Ural mountains, seen in the Chechen schoolhouse where she had been living for four months. She abandoned her job and home to search for her son, a conscript missing in action, but says she received no help from the Russian federal authorities. The federal ombudsman Oleg Mironov criticized the gross violations of human rights in Chechnya inflicted both on federal soldiers and by them. Some parliamentary deputies immediately tried to vote him out of office.

Russian Federation and these have been implemented. **Chapter 2** analyses how far international scrutiny of the Russian Federation's human rights performance has improved it.

The jurisdiction of the courts in the Russian Federation has expanded greatly since 1991, particularly in the field of civil law. This process began towards the end of President Mikhail Gorbachev's era (1985-1991). From 1989 more than 30 new laws were adopted, creating judicial remedies where previously no remedies or only administrative ones had existed.[14] The process has accelerated since then. The arrival of (legal) private enterprise, banking, and privately owned media created a need for legal ways to settle claims between individuals, and propelled civil law out of the realm of family disputes where it had been in the past.

In some suits brought by plaintiffs, courts have taken bold decisions, even when this has meant challenging powerful state agencies. A case heard by the Military Garrison in the southern city of Saratov in July 2002 is a good example. It was brought by 40 conscripts against the command of Military Unit No. 7463, demanding that the time they had spent in Chechnya be accredited double, in accordance with the law. They were told that a directive of the Defence Ministry General Staff had instructed that days spent in a military conflict zone would count extra only when the conscripts' length of service was calculated for pension purposes. The judge in the case ruled that the law had higher authority than any directive of the Defence Ministry General Staff, awarded the conscripts their double time and instructed that they be demobilized. The judgment was carried out. The conscripts themselves declined financial compensation.

According to the newspaper *Novie Izvestiia*, this was the second ruling against the Ministry of Defence that year.[15] The first had been in March in the city of Nizhnii Tagil in the Ural mountains. Both judgments against the Ministry of Defence were passed in small courtrooms in regions far away from the public eye, by courts that since 2001 have been independent of subsidies from the Ministry of Defence.[16]

However, questions about the independence of civil courts – as well as flaws in an "anti-terrorist" law – were raised during high profile cases following the October 2002 siege of a Moscow theatre. **Chapter 5** describes the unsuccessful suits brought against the Moscow City Government by relatives and hostages harmed when security forces ended the siege.

While much of civil law is new, criminal justice in the first 10 years of the Russian Federation was dispensed under laws from the Soviet era by judges who had for the most part qualified under the previous regime. Amendments were introduced to reflect constitutional guarantees of the new state. These included the presumption of innocence; the right to a public hearing; the equality of the defence and the prosecution; and access of suspects to legal counsel. However, the criminal procedures used until recently reflected the intrinsic accusatorial bias inherited from the USSR.[17] In December 2001 the Russian Federation adopted a new Criminal Procedure Code designed to be phased in over three years and to strengthen the role of the courts in the criminal justice system. **Chapter 3** examines the early impact of the new Code.

The new Criminal Procedure Code (CPC) is one of many laws adopted since 1996 and listed in the box on page 9. Some addressed problems of court organization, with a view to strengthening the independence of the courts. They gave judges tenure until the age of 65, introduced a professional judicial body to scrutinize the performance of judges, and set up a system of centralized funding under the Supreme Court. The Supreme Court has published plans to recruit up to 30,000 judges; by the end of 2001 there were 18,000. The state budget for 2003 raised spending on judges' wages and the renovation of courtrooms by 30 per cent to 25.5 million roubles (US$807,000).

Non-judicial mechanisms for protecting human rights

Both parliament and the President have developed other, non-judicial mechanisms for handling human rights questions. Article 50(3) of the Constitution gives every convicted prisoner the right to petition the President for clemency. For 10 years the Presidential Clemency Commission was one of the most effective non-judicial mechanisms of human rights protection

New laws

1991	Law on Concept of Judicial Reform
1992	Law on a Constitutional Court; Law on Court Organization
1995	Family Code
1996	Criminal Code; Civil Code
1997	Criminal-Execution Code
1998	Law on Justices of the Peace; Law on a Judicial Department of the Supreme Court
1999	Law on Military Courts
2000	Law on Status of Judges
2001	Criminal Procedure Code; Administrative Code; Labour Code
2002	Arbitration Code; Arbitration Procedure Code; and Civil Procedure Code

in the post-Soviet era. Under its civilian Chair, Anatolii Pristavkin, it annually recommended clemency for around 200 people and the commutation of nearly every death sentence. After the death penalty was ruled unconstitutional in 1999, it succeeded in having the sentences of the 716 prisoners on death row commuted to terms of imprisonment.[18] In January 2002, however, regional clemency commissions replaced the Pristavkin commission everywhere except Chechnya, where no provisions for clemency were made. Clemency ceased to be an effective institution; only 181 of the 6,600 applications made in 2002 were granted by President Vladimir Putin. **Chapter 7** describes the work of the regional clemency bodies in the context of prisoners who are serving life sentences.

Arising from Article 2 of the Constitution and the recognition it gives to individual human rights, in 1997 the State *Duma* adopted a law establishing a Federal Human Rights Commissioner — or ombudsman. Professor Oleg Mironov, a Communist Party deputy, was elected to the post in 1998. Voted in for a five-year term, the ombudsman is independent of government. The post is financed by parliament, to which the ombudsman reports annually. The ombudsman handles individual complaints against the administration, including complaints that have passed through the courts but remain unresolved. He or she can also make representations to the Constitutional Court and publish reports on their own initiative about what they perceive to be gross violations of human rights.

The federal ombudsman has powers to make
recommendations, but these are non-binding and require the
political will and action of the authorities to implement. In his
annual report for 2000, Oleg Mironov criticized gross violations
of human rights in Chechnya, both inflicted on Russian federal
troops by their commanding officers, and inflicted by Russian
federal troops on civilians.[19] The official newspaper of the State
Duma – Rossisskaia gazeta – attacked him on 4 December 2000
and some deputies moved to vote him out of office. Although he
remained in his job, none of his recommendations was
implemented.

The 89 Subjects of the Russian Federation may also elect
their own ombudsman if they so wish and at their own expense,
according to Article 5 of the Law on a Federal Human Rights
Commissioner. Twenty-two had done so at the time of preparing
this report, in regions as far apart as Kaliningrad on the Baltic
coast, Komi in the Arctic Circle and Amur on the Pacific
seaboard.[20] Their mandates vary slightly, but all handle
individual complaints against the local administration, report to
the regional parliament on the way the administration is
implementing its laws, and have statutory powers to access
documents and enter premises. All make recommendations for
improvement. The ombudsman for Tatarstan, a largely Muslim
republic on the Volga river, has the widest mandate. He must
ensure that international standards are applied within the
republic and may bring cases before the Constitutional Court of
Tatarstan. There is no regional ombudsman in the Chechen
Republic. At the time of writing this report, the regional
ombudsmen had published many recommendations in reports,
but few had been implemented.[21]

The success of each ombudsman depends partly on the
support he or she receives from parliament. Because they have no
federal law guaranteeing their status, ombudsmen in the regions
are in a shaky position, especially if they challenge their local
governor head-on. This may explain why on at least two occasions
an ombudsman in one region has addressed human rights
problems in another. In 1997, for instance, the Saratov
ombudsman addressed the Governor of Sverdlovsk Region about
police brutality against demonstrators in Yekaterinburg. In 2002,

Anatolii Pristavkin, a novelist and head of the national Clemency Commission, seen in the Commission's chamber in 1997. Under him, the Commission was one of the most effective means of human rights protection in the 1990s, securing the commutation of all death sentences in 1999. In 2002 the Commission was replaced by 88 regional ones, with no clear guidelines for their work.

the Kaliningrad ombudswoman raised the problem of ill-treatment of prisoners in Perm Region with the federal authorities.

Governmental human rights bodies were a common feature of the Soviet era, set up with a loose mandate to focus on a specific theme and with no powers of enforcement. Once the political reason for their creation had passed, they tended to vanish without trace.[22]

Two presidential human rights commissions are operating at present. One is a standing advisory commission to the President, based in Moscow. The other, a "special commission", has been based in the Chechen Republic since 2000, under President Putin's Special Representative on Human Rights and Freedoms in Chechnya — initially Vladimir Kalamanov and now Abdul-Khakim Sultygov. Several experts from the Council of Europe in Strasbourg, France, have been attached to this office, under an agreement reached with the Russian Federation's Foreign Ministry in March 2000. The task of the office is to monitor the human rights situation in the republic, and much of the special commission's time and effort has been spent processing complaints from people whose relatives have "disappeared" in Chechnya at the hands of Russian federal forces, and forwarding the complaints to the authorities for investigation and prosecution.[23]

Although the office has been in existence throughout most of the second conflict in Chechnya, it has had little impact on the climate of impunity. Few if any cases have resulted in prompt, effective and impartial investigations by the prosecuting authorities, including into the fate and whereabouts of people who have "disappeared".

© AP

Parliamentarian Galina Starovoitova was shot dead in the doorway of her St Petersburg home in November 1998, one of many political assassinations since 1991. Her murder has not been solved.

Limits of the law

The law has extended its reach in the Russian Federation, but flaws in the way it is applied mean that it still offers little protection to many people. This is a general problem for anyone living in the Russian Federation, but some people are especially far from the protection of the law, including members of ethnic minorities, women and children. The particular problems faced by children with mental disability and people in prisons in terms of protecting their rights and accessing justice are discussed in **Chapters 6** and **7**.

A wide spectrum of political violence has run alongside the evolution of legal institutions, and fallen outside their reach. Public figures have been assassinated — in the street, in their homes and at work — including eight members of the federal parliament killed by unknown assailants since the new State *Duma* was convened in 1994. Journalists investigating stories of regional or central corruption have been another target. Businesspeople have also been murdered, often when shares were being privatized or companies were changing ownership. In most of these cases, those responsible for the killings have not been prosecuted. Some cases have not even been investigated. The number of such unpunished killings since 1991 suggests that brute force pays for certain people – and deeply undermines the rule of law.[24]

Political violence and continuing problems in the justice system show that despite the strides made by the Russian Federation since 1991, much still needs to be done to protect people's fundamental human rights and to ensure that everyone has an effective remedy if their rights are violated.

Chapter 2: International systems of redress and their limitations

The Russian Federation is a member of the UN, the Organization for Security and Co-operation in Europe (OSCE) and the Council of Europe, and has undertaken to respect, protect and ensure international norms guaranteeing a wide range of human rights.

People living in the country should benefit in at least three ways:

1. Under the 1993 Constitution, international human rights treaties to which the Russian Federation is a party are now incorporated into the country's legal system, and should prevail over domestic law.

2. If domestic remedies fail them, they can now bring cases against their government to international bodies such as the (UN) Human Rights Committee, the (UN) Committee against Torture, and the European Court of Human Rights. Rulings of the European Court are binding and can include orders for payment of compensation to people whose rights under the European Convention on Human Rights (ECHR) have been violated.

3. International bodies and mechanisms are monitoring and reporting on the implementation of human rights treaties in the Russian Federation.

However, the Russian Federation has set strict limits on its cooperation with the international human rights community.

*   In 2001 it said it would not consider itself to be bound by the resolution passed by the UN Commission on Human Rights at its 57th Session and requested that "no reference be made to it in future". The resolution, which strongly condemned "all terrorist activities and attacks" and breaches of international humanitarian law by Chechen fighters, also strongly condemned the use of disproportionate and indiscriminate force and violations of human rights and humanitarian law by Russian federal forces, including "disappearances", extrajudicial executions and torture.[25] The resolution called,

International obligations

The Russian Federation has promised to uphold many international human rights standards. The UN norms include:

- International Covenant on Civil and Political Rights and its (first) Optional Protocol;
- Convention on the Elimination of All Forms of Discrimination against Women;
- International Convention on the Elimination of All Forms of Racial Discrimination;
- Convention against Torture and Other Cruel, Inhuman or Degrading Treatment or Punishment;
- International Covenant on Economic, Social and Cultural Rights;
- Convention on the Rights of the Child.

Council of Europe treaties include:

- European Convention for the Protection of Human Rights and Fundamental Freedoms;
- European Convention for the Prevention of Torture and Inhuman or Degrading Treatment or Punishment;
- Framework Convention for the Protection of National Minorities.

among other things, for the establishment of a national independent commission of inquiry to investigate alleged violations of human rights.

- In December 2002 the Russian Federation refused to extend the OSCE Assistance Group mission in the Republic of Chechnya unless it would work only on relief issues. The OSCE refused and left, because its mandate also included human rights and working towards a peaceful solution to the conflict. Its international staff had returned to Chechnya only in June 2001, after being evacuated in December 1998 in a worsening security situation.
- As of April 2003, the Russian Federation has refused to authorize publication of any of the 10 reports and recommendations made by the European Committee for the Prevention of Torture (CPT) after it visited places where people are deprived of their liberty. It is the only one of the Council of Europe's 44 member states that are party to the European Convention for the Prevention of Torture and

Inhuman or Degrading Treatment or Punishment that has yet to agree to do so. On 10 July 2001 the CPT made a public statement about the Russian Federation's failure to cooperate – only its third such statement in the 13 years that the CPT has been making visits in member states.

- At the time of writing, the Russian Federation has failed to abolish the death penalty in peacetime. It has also not yet ratified Protocol No. 6 to the ECHR, although this was a commitment it had agreed to fulfil by 1999 when it joined the Council of Europe.[26]
- The Russian Federation has maintained reservations to the ECHR, which it ratified in 1998. These mean that some of the country's procedures for arrest and detention – that fall below the standards of the ECHR – remain outside the scrutiny of the European Court of Human Rights.[27]

This chapter examines to what extent people living on Russian Federation territory have enjoyed the three main benefits that belonging to the international human rights community should have brought them – domestic applicability of international human rights guarantees; international remedies; and international monitoring.

Domestic applicability of international standards

All of the Russian Federation's obligations under international human rights treaties are directly applicable in domestic law. Individuals should be able to invoke them in a court of law, and courts and other public authorities should be applying them directly in the course of their normal work. This section looks at two areas – extraditions, and the war in Chechnya – where the Russian Federation authorities have not been applying international standards at home. Other areas where international standards are not being applied are covered later in the report.

Since its establishment, the Russian Federation has regularly extradited people to countries without first seeking assurances that they will not be tortured or sentenced to death. These extraditions have usually involved people from the Commonwealth of Independent States – formerly fellow republics

Extradition to Tajikistan

Saidamir Karimov, a Tajik from the Afghan border, came to Moscow on 20 April 2001 to start a job. He was arrested and extradited to Tajikistan on 14 May at the request of Tajik authorities investigating the murder of the former Deputy Interior Minister, Habib Sanginov. Although murder is a capital offence in Tajikistan, the Russian Federation authorities asked for no assurances that Saidamir Karimov would not be sentenced to death.

Saidamir Karimov was one of seven people charged with the murder. Six were convicted solely on the testimony of the seventh, who later retracted his evidence in court. According to an international observer who monitored the trial, this man announced at the hearing on 26 February 2002: "I say officially that I slandered every one of the accused, because I was forced to." He claimed he had been raped with a truncheon and other objects, and tortured with electric shocks. The court discounted this claim on the grounds that it had not been submitted on paper through the procuracy.

Saidamir Karimov consistently denied any involvement in the murder and was supported by 13 witnesses who had seen him at home at the time of the crime, helping his mother to water her land. He was told that his mother would be detained too if he did not agree to sign a prepared statement. He signed it.

Saidamir Karimov and his co-defendants claimed in court that they had been tortured in detention, with beatings and electric shocks to the anus, genitals, fingers, nose and ears. In a televised speech which was broadcast nationwide days before the trial, the chief State Prosecutor described each defendant as "guilty beyond doubt". Saidamir Karimov was sentenced to death on 27 March 2002.

Fear of extradition to Turkmenistan

On 3 January 2003 the Russian Federation Security Council reportedly agreed with the State Security Council of Turkmenistan to extradite three men allegedly involved in an assassination attempt on Turkmen President Saparmurad Niyazov in November 2002.[28] The three men are the former Deputy Prime Minister of Turkmenistan, the former Turkmen Ambassador to Turkey, and a freelance journalist. Although Turkmenistan has abolished the death penalty, Amnesty International feared that the men would be ill-treated and tortured if they were extradited.

On 25 November 2002 President Niyazov's motorcade had been attacked in the Turkmen capital Ashgabat. Later that day the unharmed President accused the three men — Khudayberdy Orazov, Nurmukhammet Khanamov and Orazmukhammet Yklimov — of the attack. On 29 December the Supreme Court sentenced them *in absentia* to 25 years' imprisonment, which was increased to life imprisonment the next day by the supreme legislature.

© Heidi Bradner/Panos Pictures

Scene of devastation in Grozny, Chechnya, 2000. Civilians seeking redress for violations of their rights had no courts to turn to in Chechnya at this time.

of the USSR – at first from the Caucasus but now increasingly from the Central Asian states. On average Amnesty International has learned of up to five cases a year, but believes the true figure may be higher: some cases only come to light afterwards, when a death sentence has been passed in the receiving state, or reports of torture have reached Amnesty International.

The extradition of someone to a place where they may be at risk of torture or the death penalty violates the Russian Federation's obligations under Article 3 of the ECHR, and runs counter to principles and policies of the Council of Europe.

In relation to the second war in the Chechen Republic, which began in 1999, the Russian Federation has never derogated from any of the provisions of the ECHR or the ICCPR, even though "in times of war or other public emergency" states may suspend some specified obligations under these treaties "to the extent strictly required by the exigencies of the situation". Formally, therefore, the Russian Federation remains committed to guaranteeing the rights enshrined in the ECHR and ICCPR to everyone in Chechnya. In reality, its performance has been a travesty of that commitment.

Since 1999 civilians in Chechnya have suffered relentless and massive attacks by Russian federal forces, and armed attacks by Chechen fighters. Some 178,000 people have fled their homes to live in inadequate shelters in neighbouring Ingushetia. Amnesty International has researched numerous, consistent and credible reports that Russian forces have been responsible for widespread human rights violations such as mass killings of civilians, "disappearances" and torture, including rape. The 2002 Amnesty International report *The Russian Federation – Denial of justice* describes in detail the scale of the human rights abuses perpetrated.[29]

Some offences in Chechnya have been swiftly remedied. The media has carried reports of the prosecution of Russian federal soldiers for firing on colleagues, and of trials of Chechen field commanders charged with "terrorist" offences. However, prosecutions of federal troops for serious violations of human rights or humanitarian law remain few and far between.

The war effectively destroyed much of Chechnya's infrastructure – including by 2000 its schools, prisons and courts. In its 2001 Public Statement, the CPT referred to "the palpable climate of fear" it encountered there. It said, "[M]any people who had been ill-treated and others who knew about such offences were reluctant to file complaints to the authorities. There was the fear of reprisals at local level and a general sentiment that, in any event, justice would not be done."[30]

Civilians in the Chechen Republic have been stripped of rights central to the ICCPR and the ECHR, including the rights to life, liberty, security, respect for private and family life, protection of property and freedom of expression. They have had no protection against discrimination and torture, and have been denied the right to a fair trial and an effective remedy at national level.

In 2001 the authorities opened investigations into 46 cases at the insistent request of intergovernmental organizations. On 6 March 2003 a leading military procurator, Anatolii Savenkov, announced that a total of 168 servicemen were under investigation for crimes committed against civilians and that judgment had been passed in 50 cases, but he gave no details of either the investigations or the judgments.[31] The trial of Colonel

Yury Budanov that began in the Black Sea port of Rostov-on-Don in February 2001 continued throughout 2002, with constant adjournments to assess his mental health. At the end of 2002 he was relieved of criminal responsibility on grounds of "temporary insanity". The verdict was annulled by the Supreme Court, however, and a retrial ordered for April 2003. Yury Budanov had been charged with the abduction and murder of a young Chechen woman, Kheda Kungaeva, in 2000.[32]

International remedies

When domestic remedies fail, justice can now be sought before international and regional bodies. Six cases relating to alleged human rights violations in the context of the conflict in Chechnya were registered and declared admissible by the European Court of Human Rights in January 2003. All six applicants allege that Russian federal troops violated their rights or the rights of their relatives in Chechnya in 1999-2000. They claim that their rights to life (Article 2); to protection against torture and inhuman or degrading treatment (Article 3); to an effective remedy (Article 13); and to protection of their property (Article 1 of Protocol No. 1) were violated.[33] All the applicants are citizens of the Russian Federation who lived in Chechnya and are now in Ingushetia.

Magomed Khashiev and Roza Akaeva allege that their relatives were tortured and unlawfully killed by soldiers in Grozny at the end of January 2000. A criminal investigation was opened in May 2000 and suspended and reopened several times. The culprits were never identified. The complainants say they have had no access to effective remedies at national level and allege violations of Articles 2, 3 and 13 of the ECHR.

Medka Isaeva, Zina Yusupova and Libkan Bazaeva allege that Russian military aircraft indiscriminately bombed civilians leaving Grozny in October 1999. Medka Isaeva was injured and her two children and daughter-in-law were killed. Zina Yusupova was wounded and Libkan Bazaeva's car containing the family's possessions was destroyed. A criminal investigation into the bombing started in May 2000 but was later closed. The women appealed against the closure to a military court in Rostov-on-Don and their appeal is still pending. They too claim

Strasbourg rulings

At the time of writing, 20 complaints from the Russian Federation had been registered with the European Court of Human Rights in Strasbourg and judgment passed in the first three.

On 7 May 2002, in *Burdov v Russia*, the Court found that the claimant's rights under the ECHR had been violated and awarded him €3,000 compensation, a sum the government has paid. Anatolii Burdov was entitled to a sickness pension for work he did during the Chernobyl nuclear disaster in 1986. He stopped receiving it because the Shakhtyi Social Security Service claimed it was short of funds. A local court instructed the authorities to pay, but its ruling was ignored. The European Court of Human Rights found that Anatolii Burdov's rights to protection of his property and to a fair trial had been violated.[34] The Court said that execution of a judgment is an integral part of a fair trial.

In a final judgment adopted on 15 October 2002 in the case of *Kalashnikov v Russia*, the Court found that the claimant's rights to a fair trial within a reasonable time, and his right to be protected from torture and inhuman or degrading treatment or punishment had been violated and awarded him €5,000 compensation and €3,000 costs and expenses, which the government paid (see also **Chapter 7**).[35] Valerii Kalashnikov had been detained for nearly five years on an embezzlement charge in Magadan Region, in a cell that was designed for eight prisoners but held 24.

In February 2003, in *Posokhov v Russia*, the Court concluded that there had been violations of the rights of the claimant, a customs officer from the southern port of Taganrog, and awarded him €500 compensation. Sergei Posokhov had been tried by a panel of three judges in 1996 and convicted of "abusing his position" and "abetting the avoidance of customs duties". Sergei Posokhov appealed on the grounds that two of the judges had served longer than legally permitted and were not on the official register of lay judges. His appeal was rejected as were two further attempts to have his case reviewed. The European Court of Human Rights found that Sergei Posokhov's right to a fair trial had been violated because the court that convicted him could not be regarded as "a tribunal established by law".[36]

they have had no access to effective remedies at national level and allege violations of their rights under Articles 2, 3 and 13 of the ECHR, as well as Article 1 of Protocol No. 1 on the protection of property.

Zara Isaeva alleges that indiscriminate bombing of the village of Katyr-Yurt on 4 February 2000 by federal troops killed her son and three nieces. After the European Court of

Human Rights had registered her complaint and communicated it to the Russian federal authorities for their comment, a criminal investigation was opened in September 2000, but later closed. An appeal against this decision is pending before a military court in Rostov-on-Don. Zara Isaeva claims that her relatives' right to life was violated and that she has had no effective remedy at national level, and invokes Articles 2 and 13 of the ECHR.

Given the scale of violations reported in Chechnya, the acceptance as admissible of six cases by the European Court of Human Rights may seem paltry. However, if the Court rules the cases founded and awards compensation to the victims, it will send an important moral, legal and financial signal to the Russian Federation authorities. Decisions on the admissibility of other complaints from Chechnya registered at the Court were pending at the time of preparing this report.

Since 1992, 21 individual complaints have been lodged with the (UN) Human Rights Committee, alleging that rights under the ICCPR have been violated by the authorities in the Russian Federation. To date, the Committee has upheld the complaints in two of these cases. Yelena Lantsova complained on behalf of her

The European Court of Human Rights in Strasbourg. The Court has ordered the Russian Federation government to pay financial compensation to victims, and the authorities have complied. In January 2003 the Court accepted its first six complaints from Chechnya, covering loss of property, torture, arbitrary executions, and the lack of an effective remedy.

son who died in the Matrosskaia Tishina remand prison in Moscow. In March 2002 the Human Rights Committee concluded that the authorities had violated his right to life and his right to be treated with humanity and respect for his inherent dignity in custody – under Articles 6 and 10(1) of the ICCPR respectively.

Dmitrii Gridin convinced the Committee in July 2000 that he had been convicted of rape in a trial that violated his right to be presumed innocent until proven guilty by a court, and his right to have adequate time and facilities to prepare a defence. These rights are protected under Article 14 of the ICCPR.[37]

The Russian Federation has recognized the competence of the Human Rights Committee to determine whether it has violated the ICCPR or not in regard to cases filed by individuals, through its status as a party to the (first) Optional Protocol to the ICCPR. It also undertook to ensure the rights recognized by the ICCPR to all individuals within its territory or subject to its jurisdiction. In cases where the Committee determines a violation has occurred, the Russian Federation has undertaken to provide an effective remedy.

International monitoring

In February 1995 the Parliamentary Assembly of the Council of Europe interrupted consideration of the Russian Federation's application to join the Council of Europe because of its war in the Chechen Republic.[38] The conduct of Russian federal forces during the conflict was judged to be incompatible with membership of a body committed to respect for human rights, the rule of law and democratic pluralism. Consideration was resumed in September 1995 on the grounds that Russia was "henceforth committed to finding a political solution and that alleged and documented human rights violations were being investigated".[39] By the time the second war in Chechnya began in 1999, the Russian Federation was already a Council of Europe member.

It was hoped that the Russian Federation's membership of the Council of Europe would assist in raising its respect for human rights, partly through constructive engagement. Amnesty International acknowledges that there have been improvements in some areas, but serious and widespread human rights

© Martin Adler/Panos Pictures

violations by Russian federal forces in Chechnya persist, and the domestic remedies available remain ineffective.

Raisa Kachuri comforts her mother after a gas explosion caused by shrapnel destroyed their home in Grozny, Chechnya.

Since the attacks in the USA on 11 September 2001, the Russian Federation's portrayal of the conflict in Chechnya as part of the international "war on terrorism" has found resonance among some members of the international community. In April 2002 at its 58th Session, the UN Commission on Human Rights narrowly voted against a resolution expressing concern at serious violations of human rights in Chechnya. Amnesty International issued a press release saying that the UN body had effectively turned a blind eye to egregious human rights violations committed with impunity by Russian forces against a largely defenceless civilian population. These violations include extrajudicial executions, "disappearances" and torture, including rape.[40] It added that in failing to pass the resolution the Commission had effectively endorsed Russian misconduct in Chechnya. The Commission also voted against a resolution on Chechnya at its 59th session.[41]

In November 1999, addressing the question of the war in Chechnya, the Bureau of the Council of Europe's Parliamentary Assembly said that, "persistence in violations could put under question the Russian Federation's continuing participation in the Parliamentary Assembly and in the Council of Europe generally". When the violations persisted, they were monitored by the Council of Europe across a broad front, including by its Secretary General; the CPT; the Parliamentary Assembly; and its Commissioner for Human Rights.

The war in Chechnya has been the longest and bloodiest conflict in Europe since 1999. While committing gross violations there, the Russian Federation has remained formally committed to the values of the ICCPR and ECHR. In these circumstances, Amnesty International regrets that the UN's political body – the Security Council – has chosen to remain silent on the war. It also regrets that member states of the Council of Europe have not yet sought to have the Russian Federation held to account for gross violations committed in the context of the conflict in Chechnya before the European Court of Human Rights, by lodging an inter-state complaint against the Russian Federation. On 2 April 2003 the Parliamentary Assembly of the Council of Europe said: "Lamentably, no member state or group of member states has yet found the courage to lodge an inter-state complaint" against the Russian Federation and called on member states to consider doing so.[42]

To date, 21 states have lodged applications with the European Court of Human Rights or, until it was disbanded in November 1998, with the European Commission on Human Rights. The first was Greece, which brought a complaint against the United Kingdom in 1956 for alleged breaches of the Convention on Cyprus.[43] In June 1999, shortly before the second war in Chechnya began, two more inter-state complaints were pending before the Court.[44] No inter-state applications, however, have been lodged against the Russian Federation, despite the scale and duration of the violations it has committed against civilians in Chechnya.

In April 2003 the Parliamentary Assembly adopted Recommendation No. 1600 (2003), which said:

> *"...efforts undertaken so far by all actors involved, starting with the Russian Federation Government, administration and judicial system, but also*

including the Council of Europe and its members states, have failed dismally to improve the human rights situation and ensure that past human rights violations, and in particular war crimes, are adequately prosecuted.

"If the efforts to bring to justice those responsible for human rights violations are not intensified, and the climate of impunity in the Chechen Republic prevails, [the Parliamentary Assembly recommends that the Committee of Ministers] consider proposing to the international community the setting up of an ad hoc tribunal to try war crimes and crimes against human rights committed in the Chechen Republic."[45]

On the evidence of the past 12 years, the Russian Federation's acceptance of international human rights standards has not, by any means, meant overall protection for the human rights of people within its jurisdiction. It has, however, opened up the prospect of new remedies – at local and international level – when those rights were violated. Experience shows that these remedies have been real only when they were scrupulously monitored and enforced by the international community and respected by the Russian Federation. When they were not, fundamental rights have been disregarded – like the rights of civilians caught up in the war in Chechnya, and of suspects facing extradition to states that use torture and the death penalty – and the Russian Federation has failed to account for these violations.

Chapter 3: A new look at 'innocence'

At the close of the Soviet era in 1990, the courts were reportedly acquitting 0.3 per cent of the people who came before them. In France for the same year the acquittal rate was reported to be 10 per cent.[46] Although the scope and caseload of courts in the Russian Federation has grown since 1991, the acquittal rate has stayed the same, according to Ministry of Justice figures for 2001.[47]

Taken at face value, this conviction rate might suggest that victims of crime in the Russian Federation have had almost automatic redress. Legal reformers within the Russian Federation discount this interpretation and attribute the high conviction rate to an intrinsic bias in the criminal justice system and a presumption of guilt stamped through the Criminal Procedure Code (CPC) that was in use until July 2002.

Under the old CPC, suspects were invariably deprived of their liberty and could remain in detention for months or even years with no right of access to a court or a defence lawyer until state investigators deemed their case was complete and ready to go to court. During this long pre-trial phase, detainees were exclusively in the hands of the agencies bringing the case against them: the procuracy and bodies such as the Ministry of Internal Affairs, which also administered the police cells and remand prisons where the detainees were held. Outside this closed circle, suspects had no right of face-to-face contact with anyone.

Amnesty International and other human rights organizations inside the Russian Federation and elsewhere documented reports of ill-treatment and torture before trial that were commonplace under the old CPC.[48] Since 1998, when control of the prison system was transferred to the Ministry of Justice,[49] Amnesty International has continued to document torture of suspects in police cells, which remain under the control of the Ministry of Internal Affairs.[50]

Under the old CPC, suspects had little chance of release – unless another suspect came to light for the same offence. They also had no remedy through the national courts if they had been wrongfully detained, no matter how long their detention.[51]

Study reveals unfair trials

When lawyers from Krasnoiarsk University in central Siberia studied local criminal courts from 1 January to 30 June 2000, they interviewed 148 defence lawyers; 173 recently convicted prisoners (male and female); officials from the procuracy, courts and the investigation section of the Internal Affairs Department; and scanned the press.[52] They concluded that suspects were denied a prompt, public and fair trial and had no effective remedy if they were ill-treated. It is unlikely that the violations they noted differed greatly from elsewhere in the 89 Subjects of the Russian Federation as they were studying the way the courts were applying federal law, not local law.

The Krasnoiarsk researchers learned that for most people the most powerful symbol of the court was the metal cage surrounding the defendant's dock. The study also found that:

- full public access to hearings was rare because the hearings were not announced in time, the rooms were too small, or judges refused to let people in "because the court was not a cinema";
- trials usually lasted months or years because of a shortage of judges or the non-appearance of witnesses, and the accused were normally kept in prison throughout;
- defence lawyers participated in only 80 per cent of trials and were usually appointed by the court, not the accused;
- in only 4 per cent of cases did defence counsel take part from the time of arrest;
- over 70 per cent of lawyers said that investigators hindered meetings with their clients; most believed that their consultations were secretly taped;
- over 30 per cent of convicted prisoners claimed they had confessed in police detention as a result of physical or psychological torture. Some defence lawyers said they had been unable to get the procuracy or the court – the two bodies formally charged with identifying and adjudicating cases of alleged ill-treatment – to investigate these claims.

Among hundreds of cases that Amnesty International documented, police officers were demoted for ill-treating and torturing suspects in a tiny minority of cases, and even fewer were prosecuted.

International standards

When the Russian Federation ratified the European Convention on Human Rights (ECHR) in May 1998, it accepted certain standards for what constitutes an arrest that is lawful and a trial that is fair. The full text of Articles 5 and 6 of the ECHR is given in **Appendix I** of this report, but some relevant points are summarized here.

Firstly, there is a presumption of *liberty*, according to Article 5. It foresees the possibility of detaining suspects only as an exceptional measure that is permissible only in certain expressly and narrowly defined circumstances. This list of circumstances is exhaustive and cannot be added to.[53]

Secondly, people in detention have a number of specific rights that were previously lacking in the criminal justice procedures of the Russian Federation.

- Suspects are to be told promptly in a language they understand the reasons for their arrest, and of any charge against them (Article 5(2)).
- Anyone arrested or detained in connection with a criminal charge must be brought promptly *in person* before a court or another competent judicial authority (Article 5(3)).
- Anyone detained in connection with a criminal offence must be tried within a reasonable time or be released pending trial. Release may be conditional on guarantees to appear for trial (Article 5(3)).
- Anyone deprived of their liberty has the right to take proceedings before a court to challenge the legality of their detention. The court shall make this determination speedily and order release if the detention is not lawful (Article 5(4)).
- Anyone whose rights under Article 5 are violated shall have an enforceable right to compensation (Article 5(5)).

People charged with criminal offences also have *rights* that under Russian federal procedures were previously regarded as *possibilities* only, to be granted or withheld at the discretion of the investigator or the court. Defendants have, for example, the right to:

- be informed promptly and in detail in a language they understand of the nature and cause of the charge being brought (Article 6(3)(a));
- have adequate time and facilities to prepare a defence (Article 6(3)(b));
- defend themselves in court in person, or be defended by a lawyer; where this is beyond their purse, they also have the

© Kommersant/Ivan Shapovalov

right to have free legal aid when the interests of justice require it (Article 6(3)(c));

- question or have questioned witnesses for the prosecution and to call witnesses for the defence (Article 6(3)(d));
- have the assistance of an interpreter free of charge if they cannot understand or speak the language being used in the court (Article 6(3)(e)).

People charged with criminal offences are also entitled to expect that:

- their trial should be fair, held within a reasonable time before an independent and impartial court and, except in narrowly defined circumstances, in public (Article 6(1));
- they will be presumed innocent, until they are proved guilty according to law (Article 6(2)).

An 18-year-old man awaits sentencing in a court in Moscow Region in November 2002, having spent the proceedings inside a metal cage in the courtroom. All male defendants have their heads shaved like convicts. International observers have said such practices prejudice the right to be presumed innocent until convicted by a court.

The Russian Federation had accepted similar obligations as a party to the International Covenant on Civil and Political Rights (ICCPR). The difference since 1998 is that its performance has been opened to the scrutiny of the European Court of Human Rights (see **Chapter 2**). If that Court finds that the rights of detainees or suspects under the ECHR have been violated, it could order the Russian Federation to pay financial compensation to the victim. If such violations are based on laws in force, it would be necessary for the Russian Federation to amend them in order to avoid violations in the future.

When the Russian Federation ratified the ECHR it excepted itself from obligations under provisions of Articles 5(3) and 5(4), until certain legal reforms had taken place. Without major changes to the criminal procedure in force in 1998 it could not ensure that people who were detained in connection with a criminal or military offence would be brought promptly before a judge to challenge the legality of their detention. Nor could it guarantee that their detention was ordered by a court. It also could not guarantee detainees a trial within a reasonable time or their release.

Significant features of the Russian Federation's criminal justice system were thereby closed off from the scrutiny of the European Court of Human Rights. All other aspects, however, were laid open to it.

Impact of the new Criminal Procedure Code

Since 1998 the Russian Federation has been caught in a situation where it was using very low standards of criminal procedure in its domestic law, but had to answer to much higher ones at the (UN) Human Rights Committee and the European Court of Human Rights. For instance, some 6,500 complaints against the country reached the European Court of Human Rights between 1998 and July 2001, most of them involving aspects of Articles 5 and 6 of the ECHR.[54] One outcome of this tension between domestic and international law was that work on a new Criminal Procedure Code (CPC), begun in the early 1990s, was brought rapidly to a conclusion, and in December 2001 the new CPC was adopted.

The State *Duma* envisaged that the new CPC would be phased in slowly, starting from 1 January 2003, and a timetable was laid down in the law on implementing it.[55] Court supervision of arrests was to be introduced last among the reforms, from 1 January 2004 onwards, with no completion date in view. A judgment of the

Timetable for new Code

1 July 2002	Judicial review of arrests within 48 hours introduced. Court approval required for conducting searches, confiscating property, and freezing bank accounts and obtaining confidential information from them.
1 January 2003	A panel of three professional judges must hear serious and especially serious criminal cases, replacing hearings in the presence of a single judge.
1 January 2003	The presence of a prosecutor obligatory at all criminal trials. The case for the prosecution must be argued in adversarial conditions, and no longer assumed.
1 January 2003	A system of Justices of the Peace introduced to handle petty offences. This is intended to ease the caseload of ordinary courts and make trials more prompt.
1 January 2004	Trial by jury to be introduced in all the Subjects of the Federation (except for the Chechen Republic). Originally this was scheduled to begin on 1 January 2003, but only 67 of the 89 Subjects had established juries by that date.
1 January 2007	Trial by jury to be introduced in the Chechen Republic.

Constitutional Court, however, turned this sequence back to front and accelerated the pace of implementation.

The Constitutional Court ruled on 14 March 2002 that the adoption of the new CPC marked the end of the Russian Federation's "transition period".[56] Any further delay in providing detainees with access to a court within 48 hours of their detention would therefore amount to a violation of Article 2 of the Constitution and the Russian Federation's obligations under the ECHR (Article 5) and the ICCPR (Article 9). The Constitutional Court instructed that from 1 July 2002 previous criminal procedures would lose their legal force, and judicial supervision of arrests must come into force, 18 months earlier than foreseen by legislators.

Statistics on the impact of three months of this reform had just become public at the time of preparing this report. They had been compiled by the Ministry of Justice and the Procuracy General, and cover the period from 1 July to 30 September 2002.

A striking number of people were released from detention after courts decided they had been arrested without sufficient grounds. In the three months, 3,000 detainees were freed straight from the court. According to the Ministry of Justice, this was 1,000 more than were released in the whole of 2001.

Law enforcement agents also appear to have arrested and detained fewer people over this period, perhaps because they knew that their actions would face judicial scrutiny. The Procuracy General said that the monthly figure for arrests dropped from 23,000 to 10,000. The number of new criminal cases opened also fell – by 20 per cent compared with the same period in 2001.

On first soundings, judicial supervision of arrest appears to have offered suspects some redress against wrongful detention. The information available so far does not indicate if it has also helped to identify ill-treatment of suspects or punish the people responsible for it. Such information – if any – is likely to emerge later, and through sources other than the Procuracy General and the Ministry of Justice. It is possible too that the likelihood of ill-treatment may have diminished during the probationary period of the new CPC. Any potential perpetrators would have been aware of the intense interest outside agencies were showing in the detention of suspects.

Although it is not possible yet to judge the impact that judicial supervision of arrests may have in the long term in preventing torture and ill-treatment of suspects, it has had an unforeseen beneficial impact on average conditions of imprisonment experienced by detainees awaiting trial. By January 2003 the population of detainees awaiting trial had dropped to 130,000 – its lowest since the late 1980s, according to Ministry of Justice statistics. As a result, the Ministry says, in 33 of the 89 Subjects of the Federation detainees for the first time have access to the four square metres of space they are entitled to by law. Average space for detainees in the remaining 56 Subjects has risen to 3.5 square metres. Overcrowding had previously reached such proportions in remand prisons in major cities that detainees there had only 0.2 square metres of space each. It is possible that they still do, given that the Ministry of Justice figures are based on averages and cover only a three-month period.

© Sean Sprague/Panos Pictures

The first impact of the new reform is, therefore, undoubtedly positive. However, Amnesty International believes that judicial supervision of arrests should be assessed over a much longer period and in combination with the other reforms anticipated in the new CPC. For one thing, Amnesty International is concerned that resistance to the change may emerge over time from powerful agencies such as the procuracy and the Ministry of Internal Affairs, which have been forced to surrender their powers to the courts – something they opposed throughout the whole process of drafting the new code. Secondly, it is possible that all the agencies involved in this new procedure – including the courts – have been performing according to the letter of the law for the first three months because of the scrutiny they faced. If the courts become less vigilant over time, the new procedure will offer suspects no real protection against wrongful arrest or ill-treatment.

Subjective factors could also jeopardize the success of the new CPC. Amnesty International's research indicates that very few people within the Russian Federation's criminal justice system at the moment genuinely subscribe to the presumption

Lawyers learning jury trial procedures at the Russian Academy of Jurisprudence, Moscow. Jury trials are in the processs of being introduced for serious crimes under the new Criminal Procedure Code, but will only be introduced in Chechnya in 2007.

of innocence. This is true not only of officials from the procuracy and the Ministries of Justice and Internal Affairs, but also of judges and even defence lawyers. There is a perception that any defendant acquitted by a jury, or any suspect released by a court, is a criminal who has been delivered back into society unpunished.

An interview broadcast on the *Oblako* radio program on 8 November 2002 illustrates this ambivalent attitude towards the presumption of innocence. Andrei Pokhmelkin, a defence lawyer in the Juridical Centre of the Moscow College of Advocates, was speaking about the courts' need to acquit in cases where they cannot convict. He said,

> *"In former times sending a case back for further investigation was an implicit form of rehabilitation. The court wouldn't take it upon itself to acquit somebody, but they would send [the case] back for further investigation, hinting to the investigator and the procuracy that the case wouldn't stand up and it would be better to drop it. And often the case would be closed... Getting rid of 'further investigation' is the right idea but the effect will be the opposite. The courts won't acquit more people, because for us acquittals truly are an exception. Further investigation will be out, and so the courts will convict in cases where previously they would have sent [them] back for further investigation and [they] would be closed... When the code was still being drafted we proposed that 'further investigation' should be kept in, for when either the defendant or the defence requests it, in cases when the defendants' rights had been substantially violated during the preliminary investigation, or in cases where their innocence has not clearly been established..."*

Chapter 4: Government contempt for the law

The Constitutional Court has been one of the most effective institutions for protecting human rights in the Russian Federation since 1991. It has ruled many laws and practices unconstitutional that violated international human rights norms in cases that were brought mostly by individuals, not institutions. The overwhelming majority of its rulings have taken immediate effect.

In the sphere of freedom of movement, however, its rulings have yet to bite because of the defiance of some prominent public authorities. These include the Mayor of Moscow, Yury Luzhkov.

Amnesty International believes that all public authorities should be bound by the rule of law. It urges the Russian Federation government to use the measures available to it to ensure that they implement the Constitutional Court's rulings without delay.

In defiance of the Constitutional Court

When Yury Luzhkov was campaigning for re-election as Mayor of Moscow in 2000, he told journalists who asked him about his *propiska* system that "the Russian Constitution does not apply in Moscow". He was defending the practice of controlling access to the capital by requiring people to get permission to live there.

The USSR Committee of Constitutional Supervision first ruled the *propiska* system illegal in October 1991. Since 1995 the current Constitutional Court has ruled it illegal on at least eight separate occasions, on the grounds that the need to seek "permission" to be at a particular address violates the right to freedom of movement, sojourn and residency.[57]

In 1996, after the court's first ruling, around 30 Subjects of the Russian Federation were thought to have kept some form of residency restrictions.[58] These sometimes took the form of immigration quotas — as in Stavropol Territory; or prohibitively expensive immigration procedures — as in Moscow Region; or discriminatory taxes on settlers — as in Moscow City. The

Yuri Luzhkov, the Mayor of Moscow, who declared that the Constitution "does not apply in Moscow" and has defied court rulings to abolish residence permits.

Constitutional Court ruled these restrictions illegal also in April 1996[59] and found against other residency restrictions in the years that followed.

By 2003 around 10 Subjects of the Russian Federation were thought still to restrict residency in law or in practice. These included St Petersburg, Leningrad Region and Kalingrad Region in the west; Stavropol Territory and Krasnodar Territory in the south; and Nizhnyi-Novgorod, Moscow Region and Moscow City in the central zone.

Amnesty International's report *Dokumenty! – Discrimination on grounds of race in the Russian Federation* details how registration procedures have been used discriminatively against Meshkhetian Turks living in Krasnodar Territory.[60] This report looks at how Moscow City has applied residency restrictions across a broad front, with negative consequences for human rights.

There are strict time limits for Subjects of the Russian Federation to bring their laws into line with the Constitution, and public authorities are legally bound to observe them. They are set down in a federal law adopted in 1999 – On the General Principles for Organizing the Legislative (Representative) and Executive Organs of State Power of the Subjects of the Russian Federation.[61] The law did not come into force for two years in order to allow time for regional inconsistencies to be ironed out.

Given the Constitutional Court's strong stand on the issue, Amnesty International is concerned that illegal residency restrictions in the Subjects were not eradicated during this two-year grace period. It is also disturbed that the Russian Federation authorities made no attempt to enforce compliance through the law's provisions.

© Mikhail Solovyanov/Moscow Times

The law empowers President Vladimir Putin as the "guarantor of the Constitution" to suspend any legal act he believes violates the federal Constitution, pending a court ruling on the issue.[62] If a court finds the act to be illegal, the Governor of the Subject – or the Mayor in the case of Moscow City – must take remedial action within two months, or face a formal warning from President Putin.[63] Should the Governor or Mayor then fail to do all in their power to eradicate the illegality within a month of the warning, President Putin is empowered to dismiss him or her from office.[64] The Russian Federation Supreme Court must rule on the case within 10 days if the dismissal is appealed.[65]

Tajik construction workers leaving Khimki for home ahead of deportation in November 2002. Since 2000 there has been visa-free travel for Tajiks coming to Russia. International obligations state that everyone legally within the territory of a state is entitled to move around and choose their place of residence freely.

Amnesty International knows of one case in which a regional court has already acted successfully on the basis of this law to stop an illegal practice at district level. In August 2002 Sverdlovsk regional court in the Ural mountains found that the mayoral practice of refusing to sign laws into effect violated federal legislation. The court instructed the regional parliament to adopt a new law, closing the loopholes that made the abuse possible. This was done. Previously, mayors in the region were able to ignore legislation they did not like, and so only laws that had been agreed with them beforehand took effect.

In Amnesty International's view it is time for the law to be applied comprehensively to eradicate the residency restrictions and the human rights violations they entail.

Propiska and human rights violations

The time limits set out above apply only if major abuses of human rights have arisen from the violation of the law.[66] The *propiska* system in Moscow violates international human rights obligations that form part of Russian domestic law.[67]

Article 12(1) of the ICCPR states that:

"Everyone lawfully within the territory of a State shall, within that territory, have the right to liberty of movement and freedom to choose his residence."

Inside the Moscow City limits, however, legal residence permits are available only to Muscovites and their spouses, or to people newly arrived in the capital who can afford to buy their own property.

Other human rights violations have arisen from the *propiska* system:

- ethnic minorities have been prey to constant police checks and even summary deportation from the city, with no access to a lawyer or other procedural rights;
- Moscow's homeless have been unable to get the medical help they need because they are not registered at an address and so have no access to a doctor;
- same-sex partners have been unable to live together in Moscow if one comes from outside the city; registration extends only to married incomers joining their spouse.

In the context of war in Chechnya and a perceived "terrorist threat", the *propiska* has enabled the Moscow authorities to target and collectively expel specific ethnic groups — not for any criminal offence, but on the grounds of their identity. Foreign nationals have been summarily expelled amid scenes of racial abuse and violence. This violates human rights obligations that the Russian Federation has undertaken. For example, Article 13 of the ICCPR states,

*"An alien lawfully in the territory of a State Party
to the present Covenant may be expelled
therefrom only in pursuance of a decision
reached in accordance with law and shall, except
where compelling reasons of national security
otherwise require, be allowed to submit the
reasons against his expulsion and to have his case
reviewed by, and be represented for the purpose
before, the competent authority or a person or
persons especially designated by the competent
authority."*

Nationals of the Russian Federation have also been
subjected to this treatment and expelled from the city. Most of
them, but not all, have been Chechens.

Registration in Moscow City gives access to education,
health care and social security benefits in the city. Those not
registered therefore have no access to these essential services.
The newspaper *Trud* commented on 3 August 2002:

*"Afghan families have been living in Moscow with-
out registration for 10 years. They work wherever
they can and have no access to health care and no
way to send their children to school. The federal
government knows about these illegal aliens and
their wretched situation of course, but it pretends
they don't exist."*

Nezavisimaia gazeta on 6 June 2002 reported the problems of
another unregistered group in Moscow:

*"Ambulances picked up the bodies of 860 homeless
people from the streets of Moscow in 2001, 430 of
them in winter. Most likely they died of illnesses,
not fatal ones. It's hard enough for an ordinary
Muscovite to obtain medical care... but if a
person has no residence permit — known by the
pseudonym 'registration' — what then?"*

Later in the same article, the French medical charity
Medecins Sans Frontières, which has been assisting the
homeless in Moscow for the past 10 years, said that registration
and problems of bureaucracy were greater hindrances to their
work than the Russian winter.

Discriminatory justice

A Romani woman, Svetlana Stepanova, may have fallen victim to racial stereotyping by the justice system. In May 2002 she was convicted by Taganka Inter-Municipal (District) Court in Moscow of drug dealing on an especially large scale, under Article 228(4) of the Criminal Code. The Court found that she had supplied 1.81g of heroin to a known addict in exchange for a television set, and sentenced her to six years' imprisonment. Svetlana Stepanova had no previous convictions.

Although Svetlana Stepanova cannot read or write, she was given no help to understand the charge against her, and no lawyer at the time of her arrest or during preliminary questioning in November 2000. She was accused of having supplied drugs to an addict who was taking part in a police "sting" to entrap a dealer. She has consistently denied the accusation. Two police officers, witnesses and a driver were present when the drug deal took place, but none of them could identify Svetlana Stepanova as the dealer. She was not arrested at the scene of the crime, but in her own home some time later. No trace of narcotics was discovered there.

Svetlana Stepanova has four children – all minors – but because she has no *propiska* for Moscow City, she was held in prison awaiting trial. This lasted for 18 months. During this time, her family was broken up and her children fostered separately. They are now living with her sister. For reasons that are not clear, a presidential amnesty approved in January 2002 for women prisoners with young children did not extend to Svetlana Stepanova.

Svetlana Stepanova alleges that police manhandled her when they arrested her, hit her around the head, and stole some of her possessions. None of her requests from the remand prison to see a doctor was granted, nor were her allegations of police impropriety investigated. She is now serving her sentence in a strict regime corrective labour colony in Mordovia. Her appeal to the Supreme Court was rejected later in the year.

Certain groups of people have been victims of frequent police checks, sometimes leading to expulsion from the city. In 2002, for example, Roma were targeted by Moscow police in two drives to check registration papers. In March, in an operation called "Operation *Tabor*" ("Operation Gypsy Camp"), police detained 140 Roma without registration papers and expelled them beyond the limits of Moscow Region. Their names were entered in a special card file and their fingerprints were taken before expulsion. From 10-24 July, a further 1,695 Roma without registration documents were detained in an operation called "*Tabor-2*", according to the newspaper *Vremia MN* on 30 July. Of

© Gueorgui Pinkhassov/Magnum Photos

St Petersburg police checking the identity of Roma. Two police swoops in Moscow in 2002 led to the detention of nearly 2,000 Roma, but only a handful were then prosecuted. Others were expelled from the city.

these, the detention of only 20 was prolonged because they were suspected of crimes.

Anatolii Yashkov, a Moscow police official, told the newspaper *Izvestiia* on 17 July 2002: "Gypsies have got into a new business lately – drugs. It's lucrative, a source of steady income. Women and children are being brought into the business." An International Union of Gypsies spokesperson told the newspaper that police operations that identify criminal behaviour directly with a specific ethnic group "take Russia back to the Middle Ages, or pre-war Germany".

Since November 2000 the Russian Federation has permitted visa-free travel for nationals of Belarus, Kyrgyzstan and Tajikistan because of its need for migrant labour.[68] A report on seasonal labour in the southern Volgograd Region in the official newspaper of the State *Duma, Rossisskaia gazeta*, illustrated the officially recognized economic benefits of such labour.[69] It said that in spring, Uzbeks, Tajiks, Koreans and Chinese people dominate the labour intensive farm industry in the region, and for very low pay produce crops of onions, tomatoes, cucumbers and other vegetables at four times the regional average.

However, despite such recognition of their work, once legally inside the Russian Federation, migrants from these countries still fall foul of Moscow's unconstitutional rules on registration. Most vulnerable are Tajiks, who constitute the largest group and the cheapest labour, around 80 per cent of whom work at poorly paid jobs in the construction industry or as market traders. Tajik migration officials estimate that in 2002 alone more than half a million Tajiks found jobs in the Russian Federation, most of them young men.

The 2003 Amnesty International report, *'Dokumenty!'* – *Discrimination on grounds of race in the Russian Federation*, details the physical and verbal abuse typically directed at immigrants in Moscow, particularly those with darker skins.[70] Discrimination against Tajiks intensified at the end of 2002 after an armed group, all believed to be Chechens, held hundreds of people hostage in a Moscow theatre in October (see **Chapter 5**). The Tajik newspaper *Varorud* described the atmosphere in Moscow on 11 November:

> *"Mass inspections are being conducted in markets and the examination of vehicles has been stepped up. As usual, 'dark-skinned' visitors are scapegoats... Any negative event in any Russian Region boomerangs against 'dark-skinned' people, including Tajiks. This is the reality from which there is no place to hide. This once more underlies the events in Moscow and the actions of the Russian law enforcement agencies, that will inflict new sufferings on our compatriots."*

On 20 November 2002 mass detentions of Tajiks took place in Moscow City and Moscow Region. In some cases, police publicly tore up permanent residence permits belonging to detainees. Eighty Tajiks were put in cells in the town of Serpukhov, south of Moscow, kept without food for two days, and subjected to humiliating abuse. On 22 November, 117 Tajiks were forced aboard a military aeroplane and deported to Dushanbe, the capital of Tajikistan, from Chkalov airport. On 29 November a further 73 were forced to join them.

The Foreign Ministry of Tajikistan officially protested against the deportations on 30 November. It said, "Given the

Chapter 5: Impunity under 'anti-terrorism' law

In October 2002 dozens of armed men and women, all believed to be Chechens, took hostage more than 800 people in a theatre in Moscow, and during the three-day siege killed three of their captives. In the course of the rescue operation, 50 of the hostage-takers and at least 129 hostages died – some as a result of bullet wounds; most as a result of a gas released by the security forces into the theatre.

The rescue attempt and its aftermath threw a harsh light on the authorities' attitude to the life and welfare of the civilians who were hostages. It also raised serious questions about the impunity enjoyed by officials under the 1998 Law to Combat Terrorism.

In a landmark case, 61 people attempted to sue Moscow City Government for damages under the Law to Combat Terrorism in connection with the way the authorities ended the siege. On 23 January 2003 Tverskoi Inter-Municipal (District) Court rejected the first three suits – details of which are highlighted in the text and one of the boxes below. An Amnesty International observer attended the court hearings in this case, and was present when judgment was passed on the first three suits.

Moscow theatre siege

"Today, early in the morning, an operation was conducted to free the hostages. We succeeded in doing what seemed almost impossible – in saving the lives of hundreds and hundreds of people. We showed that Russia cannot be forced to her knees. But now, first of all, I would like to address the relatives and friends of those who have perished. We could not save everyone. Forgive us. The memory of those who have died must unite us. I thank all the citizens of Russia for their endurance and unity."

President Putin, in a television address on 26 October 2002

While deeply shocked at the loss of life following the hostage-takers' actions, the circumstances that made a siege possible in

© Sergei Karpukhin/Reuters/popperfoto.com

Special forces carrying hostages out of the House of Culture theatre in Moscow. The authorities failed to arrange sufficient stretchers for the survivors or ambulances to take them to hospital. Many injured people were transported on the floors of buses with no medical attendants or outriders to clear traffic.

central Moscow, and the way it was broken up, left many people deeply disturbed about the methods used by the security forces and the attitude of the authorities.

The siege began on the evening of 23 October 2002 when 59 armed men and women took more than 800 people hostage in the House of Culture on Melnikov Street in central Moscow, during a showing of the *Nord-Ost* musical.[75] The hostages included members of the audience, the cast, the orchestra and people from private groups rehearsing in practice rooms, many of them children. The hostage-takers demanded the withdrawal of Russian federal troops from Chechnya. They said they had mined entry points to the theatre and that women among them were wearing explosives.

The siege lasted until 26 October, during which the hostage-takers shot and killed three people. One was a woman who wandered into the theatre from the street on 23 October. The hostage-takers collected the passports of everyone in the building, and threatened to kill a Major General of the Ministry of Internal Affairs who was in the theatre.[76] During the siege, hostages were given food and drink from the theatre buffet, and the orchestra pit was used as a toilet. The captors released some hostages with health problems.

In the early hours of 26 October the authorities released a soporific gas into the theatre. Within minutes *Alfa* troops (Special Group A troops attached to the Federal Security Service) stormed the building, shot dead 50 hostage-takers and evacuated the hostages, most of whom were incapable of independent movement at that time. According to Olga Karpova, a senior doctor with the Department of Operational Response of the Moscow Rescue Service, at least 37 hostages died in the theatre.[77] Some 646 were taken to hospitals and by 28 November around one in six of them had died. A total of 129 hostages are known to have lost their lives as a result of the rescue operation. A further 68 are said to be unaccounted for.[78] Lawyers bringing the civil suits allege that another 40 had died by April 2003 from complications arising from contact with the gas, but details were not available when this report went to print.

Around 400 hostages were sent for treatment at Hospital No. 13, the nearest hospital but one of the smallest, with a staff of only 50. In the ensuing delays, some patients who needed urgent treatment did not get it. Others, including Aleksei Shalnov (see box page 55), were discharged prematurely and subsequently died. Hostages were also sent to Hospitals 1, 7 and 9; Sklifosovskii First Aid Institute; Botkin Hospital; and the Military Hospital of War Veterans. Hostages suspected of colluding with the hostage-takers were sent to Hospital No. 20.

When the siege was unfolding, Amnesty International unreservedly condemned the taking of hostages and considers it to have been a deplorable act. After the siege ended, Amnesty International and others called for a thorough and independent investigation of the rescue operation.[79]

On 14 November the State *Duma* voted against setting up a parliamentary commission to investigate how the theatre siege had come to happen in the centre of Moscow and how it was

The body of a man thought to be one of the hostage-takers, lying at the entrance of the House of Culture in Moscow after it was stormed by troops on 26 October 2002. Some eyewitnesses reported that the hostage-takers were shot when they were already unconscious. Amnesty International believes they should have been brought to trial, and is concerned that among those shot there may have been people mistaken for hostage-takers because they belonged to ethnic minorities.

resolved. It also voted for laws to restrict media access to such events in future and to prohibit the return of the corpses of "terrorists" to their place of origin. In the face of international pressure and representations from the media at home, President Putin vetoed the proposed press restrictions on 25 November.

The Moscow City Government paid 100,000 roubles (about US$3,200) in compensation to relatives of hostages who had died and 50,000 roubles to each hostage who had been injured. These sums are prescribed in Article 17 of the Law to Combat Terrorism.

The fight for compensation

On 16 December the first eight claims were lodged against the Moscow City Government for moral and material damages totalling US$7.5 million. Other claims followed.

Public opinion was divided on the claims. Some commentators welcomed the fact that the claimants were insisting upon their rights. Moscow City Government said the claims would bankrupt it and push prices up in the city.

Court's impartiality questioned

Before and during hearings in the House of Culture case, lawyers and plaintiffs formally expressed no confidence in the court and petitioned to have the hearings transferred to the Russian Federation Supreme Court. They argued that the Tverskoi Inter-Municipal (District) Court could not judge their case impartially because it was dependent on the sole respondent – Moscow City Government – for a significant part of its income. A copy of the city budget was attached to the case documents.

The Court rejected the petitions, and in January 2003 dismissed the first three claims for compensation. The complainants lodged an appeal with the Moscow City Court, which was dismissed in April 2003.

The 89 Subjects of the Russian Federation are obliged to pay fixed sums each year towards the federal budget, money that goes to the Supreme Court and is used to pay for judges' salaries, court rents and new legal institutions such as Justices of the Peace. Such has been the deficit of court funding over many years that most local courts need more.

Moscow City Court also benefits from direct partial funding from Moscow City Government. Amnesty International is concerned that direct local authority subsidies of this sort can compromise the independence of the courts. While individual judges may still act impartially and with integrity, there can be no certainty in the public mind that they are doing so because of the source of their income. Courts that are independent and impartial – and seen to be so – are requirements for a fair trial under Article 6 of the ECHR and Article 14 of the ICCPR.

In the figures available to Amnesty International, the Moscow City Government has allocated 700 million roubles (around US$22.5 million) to courts within the city in the form of direct grants, as well as to the federal budget for upkeep of the federal court system for 2003. The money given locally is earmarked for heating and electricity, telecommunications, rent, work-related travel for judges, social insurance, etc.[80]

At the court hearings, the claimants thanked Moscow City Government for its donation, but said they were suing for material damages since they and their families had been left without any means of financial support as a result of the rescue attempt – either because their breadwinner had been killed or their own injuries made them unfit to work. They were also suing for moral damages because of the way they were treated by the authorities during and after the rescue operation.

At the heart of the case was the authorities' use of an unnamed gas to end the siege. The gas was later identified as

Daniil Abudallaevich Chernetsov was an usher at the House of Culture and had been married for two months when he was caught in the siege. On the first evening he telephoned his mother to reassure her he would be coming home. That was the last time she heard from him.

After the *Alfa* troops ended the siege on 26 October, Daniil Chernetsov's mother, a doctor, dashed between hospitals in the city and local morgues looking for her son, but discovered nothing. By 29 October, she told the court, she realized that something was wrong.

When she was shown photographs of bodies at the city morgues, she recognized her son only by the shape of his ears. The photograph had been taken after an autopsy.

She went to identify his body at Morgue No. 11. Daniil Chernetsov's body, which was covered in a black plastic bag, was wheeled out on a trolley. His mother asked if she could look at his hands and a small scar on his arm, but she was not allowed to. Nor was she given a death certificate when she asked for one. Later she got a copy from the local records office, but no cause of death was given on the certificate. She is still waiting to receive the results of her son's autopsy.

Daniil Chernetsov's mother still has unanswered questions. What was the cause of her son's death and why was his body hidden from her?

On 27 October the newspaper *Kommersant* reported that *Alfa* troops had mistaken several hostages for hostage-takers and had summarily shot them dead. She fears that this may have happened to her son. Daniil Chernetsov was part Russian, part Uzbek and did not look typically Slav. He was 21 when he died.

being "based on derivatives of fentanyl, a commonly used anaesthetic", by the Minister of Health, but only on 30 October 2002 — four days after the siege had ended.[81] The Minister refused to be more precise even on 11 December when faced with a parliamentary question. He said it was a "state secret".

The claimants contended that the authorities made woefully inadequate preparations for hostages caught in the gas attack, although they knew in advance what gas they were using. Fentanyl administered in large and uncontrolled doses — as it was through the theatre's air conditioning system — leads quickly to respiratory problems and to coma. Oxygen is vital within minutes, but neither this nor an antidote appeared to have been widely provided for hostages in the street outside the theatre. Hospitals earmarked to give the hostages medical treatment were not alerted to the use of fentanyl, and for several crucial hours their staff were unable to find an adequate antidote.

Yakha Khalidovna Neserkhoeva, an economist from Chechnya, had been living for many years in Moscow, where she worked in a shop. At the start of the siege the hostage-takers offered to let her leave, but she refused. She had come to see the musical with a Russian friend, and did not want to leave her alone as a hostage.

When the *Alfa* troops stormed the theatre, Yakha Neserkhoeva was arrested on suspicion of being one of the hostage-takers. She was taken – half-naked, according to witnesses – to Hospital No. 20, where suspects were being treated. Aged 43 and suffering from a heart and respiratory complaint, she had reacted extremely badly to the gas attack.

Yakha Neserkhoeva's friends and colleagues searched unsuccessfully for her. They turned to the Procurator, but he refused to accept their statement. They hired a lawyer and broadcast an appeal for her whereabouts on the radio. The Memorial human rights centre in Moscow appealed to the Procurator General to release her, since the sole grounds for her arrest was her nationality as a Chechen. She was eventually released on 5 November with no charges against her. Her lawyer is suing the newspaper *Zhizn* for slander, for publishing a prejudicial article on her case.

Although there were more than 800 hostages in the theatre, the authorities planning the rescue attempt provided few stretchers and only a handful of ambulances. Many hostages were transported in municipal buses with no outriders to accompany them through city traffic and no medical assistance on board. Some were placed on the floor of buses. Aleksandra Karpova, whose son Aleksandr was killed in the rescue attempt, told the court hearing in one of the first three suits that she saw television footage of a soldier stepping on her son's body. Because of the inadequate rescue arrangements, there were fears that many hostages suffered unnecessary and irreparable damage to their health before they could receive hospital treatment.

Relatives of hostages also claimed moral damages for the way the authorities kept them in the dark about what had happened to their loved ones. All the hostages had identification papers with names and addresses on them, but in the immediate aftermath the authorities made no attempt to contact relatives or to produce a list of casualties with their whereabouts. Photographs of the dead were produced only two days after the theatre was stormed. Relatives said that on 26 and 27 October they were forced to run between hospitals and city morgues in search of their loved ones. Several received death certificates that were incomplete, with the

Aleksei Shalnov was rehearsing with a youth orchestra in a back room of the House of Culture when the siege began. As he was recovering from bronchitis at the time, his parents had brought him to the rehearsal and were in the theatre waiting to take him home. His mother was downstairs and his father was in a waiting room, watching a closed circuit television broadcast of the musical. His father told the court he watched the hostage-takers take over the stage, but was unsure if it was part of the show. Thirty minutes of shooting followed, during which Aleksei Shalnov's mother managed to escape through a downstairs window.

Aleksei Shalnov's father remained a hostage on the theatre balcony throughout the siege and managed to visit Aleksei twice in the room where he was being held with the youth orchestra and their conductor. He could hear that Aleksei's bronchitis was growing worse on the evening of 25 October. Later that night he saw hostages below him reaching for cloths to cover their faces. He smelt nothing, but passed out and did not regain consciousness until more than 16 hours later at 9pm on 26 October.

On 27 October Aleksei Shalnov was discharged from the neurological ward of Hospital No. 2 with a clinical diagnosis saying "victim of a terrorist attack" suffering from "biochemical action". The discharge note had been wrongly dated 29 October. He was given a letter by the hospital for his local clinic recommending outpatient treatment for his liver and kidneys within two weeks. Aleksei Shalnov's father said the boy's face was dark by the time he got home and he was moving sluggishly. However, before he had a chance to go to the local clinic he became seriously ill and his parents called a doctor. He subsequently died of nephritis and hepatitis.

cause of death being given as "terrorist attack". Some were notified only days after the autopsy had taken place. Some of the claimants in the first series of suits objected that the dead hostages' citizenship had been deleted from their death certificates.

The relatives also complained about the standard of assistance for funerals provided by Moscow City Government, which they said caused them additional distress. Aleksandra Karpova told the court hearing that the coffin she was given by the city government did not fit her son and was disintegrating. Officials advised her to buy another coffin and resell them both in order to buy a decent one. This she was obliged to do.

Moscow City Government did not contest the facts put forward by the plaintiffs in court, but denied any responsibility for "moral damage" under the Civil Code. It argued that it had already met its responsibilities to relatives and hostages for material damages they had suffered. The court dismissed the first three claims, without giving reasons. The claimants appealed to the next higher court – Moscow City. It dismissed their appeals in April 2003.

The Law to Combat Terrorism

The 1998 Law to Combat Terrorism makes it virtually impossible for someone with a grievance arising from an "anti-terrorist" operation to gain redress. It exempts from liability those participating in such an operation, even if they violate human rights.

Responsibility for planning "anti-terrorist" operations lies with federal bodies – the President and the government of the Russian Federation – which may set up a command centre to tackle individual incidents, according to Article 10 of the Law. This centre would normally include representatives of the Federal State Security Service; the Ministry of Internal Affairs; the Ministry of Defence; the Federal Border Guards' Service; the External Intelligence Service; and the Service of Federal Protection – under the overall control of the President of the Russian Federation. These federal agencies can instruct local health and transport services to assist.

The Law to Combat Terrorism does not, however, ascribe any responsibility to the decision-makers for damage arising from an "anti-terrorist" operation. Material damages are to be paid by the authority where the incident happens to take place and according to fixed rouble tariffs – provisions set down in Articles 17(1) and 20 of the Law. Neither federal nor local authorities are liable under this law for "moral damage" to survivors. The only exception is for foreign nationals who suffer damages in an "anti-terrorist" operation in the Russian Federation, who may claim compensation from the federal bodies in charge of the operation.[82]

In the House of Culture case, the President and a team of federal agents were responsible for all operational aspects of the rescue attempt, including the decision to storm the building, the use of gas, the apprehension and shooting of "terrorist" suspects, the evacuation of hostages, the provision of emergency services, the handling of relatives, and information to the media.

Women hoping to catch a glimpse of their loved ones being treated at Moscow's Hospital No. 13 after the theatre siege, 27 October 2002. Around 400 survivors were brought to the hospital, which was closest to the siege but has only 50 staff. The medical staff were not told immediately what gas had been used to break up the siege. Many of their patients reportedly died because of delays in their treatment or because they were discharged too early.

At the hearing of the first series of civil suits, however, Moscow City Government was the only respondent – in accordance with the Law to Combat Terrorism. Making a gesture of wiping his hands, a member of Moscow City Government's legal team told Amnesty International, "[u]ltimately no one is responsible". This situation would apply wherever a "terrorist" siege might take place in the future.

Amnesty International has a number of serious concerns about the siege of the House of Culture and the way it was ended by the authorities.

Regrettably, the methods used to break up the siege resulted in loss of life. President Putin apologized that the "anti-terrorist" troops had not been able to rescue everyone: in fact, at least 126 more people died than at the direct hands of the hostage-takers, who had placed them in such a vulnerable situation. No one has yet been held to account for actions during and after the rescue operation, which in some cases may have violated human rights, and to Amnesty International's knowledge, no official has resigned in connection with them.

Article 21 of the Law to Combat Terrorism absolves people fighting "terrorism" of "responsibility for damage caused". Amnesty International deplores the level of impunity that this allows, and considers that no law should exonerate those responsible for human rights violations.

Respect for legality is supposed to be the principle of "anti-terrorist" operations, according to Article 2.1 of the Law to Combat Terrorism. Amnesty International is disturbed by reports that suspected hostage-takers were summarily shot, among them people who were reportedly mistaken for hostage-takers. While it is understandable that the authorities wanted to prevent the detonation of explosives believed to be in the theatre, reports suggest that the hostage-takers were already incapacitated by the fentanyl gas.

Some eyewitnesses stated that all the hostage-takers shot dead were killed when they were already unconscious. Article 23 of the Law to Combat Terrorism states, "[t]errorists must bear responsibility for their actions in accordance with the law". In this case, the shooting of people already incapacitated whom the authorities suspected were "terrorists" prevented their prosecution before a court of law. It also raises the possibility that hostages from minority ethnic groups may have been shot. Amnesty International is concerned about reports indicating that the authorities' response was neither lawful nor proportionate, as required by the Russian Federation's international obligations.

According to eyewitnesses and media photographs, the troops who broke the siege on 26 October moved freely around the theatre without breathing apparatus. This suggests that the authorities planning the rescue attempt had provided them with an antidote to fentanyl. It appears that no such forethought was given to the effect of the gas on the hostages. The absence of adequate medical equipment, staff, transport, support and information for relatives suggests an almost total disregard for members of the public. The complacency of the government and parliament about this rescue attempt is both astonishing and disturbing. Also disturbing is the fact that real remedies available to someone wronged in an "anti-terrorist" operation of this sort are virtually non-existent.

Chapter 6: Confinement of children with mental disability

The sign on the door said: "Beware! Keep out!" This was the corridor where children are kept permanently in bed. There were 27 beds in six tight rows in a ward that was clean and bright. A television was switched on over the bed of an 18-year-old woman who could speak with an Amnesty International delegate visiting the *internat* (orphanage) and was excited about the visit. She was the oldest. The others were boys and girls from the age of four who were unable to speak.

The room was silent. Three of the children had Down's Syndrome and the delegate was told the others were suffering from "imbecility" and "idiocy". As the children had been in bed all their lives, their arms and legs were wasted and their skin covered in sores. One nine-year-old boy lay curled up, the size of a four-year-old.

"It is surprising they are alive," the chief doctor mused loudly, within earshot of the children. "They are like vegetation. Their lungs and hearts work but there is nothing going on in their heads."

Between three and five children die on the ward each year — an annual death rate of more than 10 per cent. There are 205 children in *Internat Z* (not its real name), some 400 kilometres from Moscow, 30 of them suffering from epilepsy.[83]

There are 155 institutions like *Internat Z* in the Russian Federation and they are home to around 29,000 children.[84] Some of the children are orphans or from broken homes, but a significant number were born with mental disabilities and taken away from their parents. A further 19,400 children up to the age of four are living in children's homes.

There is no law passed by parliament protecting the interests of children with mental disability. They can be put into an institution through a relatively simple procedure that is regulated by a ministerial directive that has barely changed since it was adopted in the Soviet era in 1978.[85]

Often the procedure starts in the maternity ward. If a commission of doctors has diagnosed that a baby has

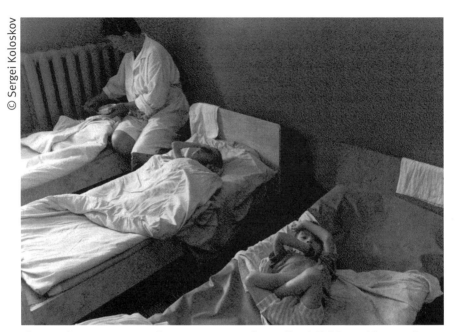

© Sergei Koloskov

Children with mental disability who are confined permanently to their beds.

abnormalities in its central nervous system that will lead to mental disability, they may recommend taking the child into state care. If the parents agree, they sign a legally binding form renouncing their parental rights. This procedure has typically been applied to babies with Down's Syndrome. When the child is older the same procedure may come into play if they are suspected of having cerebral palsy or autism. Doctors may recommend state care for children with symptoms of cerebral palsy between the ages of seven and 14 months, and for those with autism up to the age of five. At the age of four the children undergo further examination by a commission of doctors and educationalists that typically finds them "unfit to be educated" — a term recommended by a Ministry of Education Directive of 20 November 1974. This diagnosis presents a bleak picture of the future to parents.

The procedure gives enormous discretion to the hospital staff. To begin with, they do not have to show the baby to the parents. Unscrupulous staff could therefore take perfectly healthy children away from their parents without full checks or controls. In 2002 the Russian media carried reports of doctors in the east Siberian region of Irkutsk who were being prosecuted for selling healthy babies for adoption abroad.

Anna was eight years old, with lively eyes. She ran up to greet the Amnesty International delegate in *Internat Z*. She had an open hare lip and an open cleft palate. She was able to eat despite this, but could not speak. Two teeth projected through the open lip from her upper gum, disfiguring a vital face.

Back in the *internat's* office the Amnesty International delegate asked the doctor if it would be possible to operate on Anna's mouth, particularly as she was approaching a self-conscious age. The doctor doubted that with her mental disability she would survive the anaesthetic. "And, anyway, she has no awareness of herself, and in the future we foresee for her, she has no need to be self-aware. She will be living in these four walls, and then in those four walls." He gestured to an old people's home in the same complex, where Anna would go when she reached the age of 18.

Doctors in *Internat Z* and elsewhere in the mental health field refer to conditions like "oligophrenia", "imbecility" and "idiocy" that do not exist in the World Health Organization's International Classification of Diseases (IDC-10). This use of outmoded terminology poses the risk that children may be kept in homes inappropriately, and not given opportunities available to children diagnosed in a different framework.

No independent information is available to parents that might put a different light on the medical advice they are receiving. There are also virtually no social services to help parents bring up children with mental disabilities at home, so the alternative to putting their child in a state institution is immensely daunting. In his 2001 *Report on the Rights and Opportunities of the Disabled*, the Federal Human Rights Commissioner Oleg Mironov observed that "invalids" and families with disabled children are among the poorest social groups in the country.[86] Social workers and self-help groups are just beginning to find their feet in the Russian Federation and are not yet able to provide all families that need them with adequate practical support, information or equipment.

From the point of view of the child, one of the most alarming aspects of the procedure is that there is no requirement for a review of their placement. This caused concern to the UN Committee on the Rights of the Child when it considered a report from the Russian Federation in 1999.[87] Nothing, however, has been done about it. The current procedures do not give parents even the opportunity to request a review.

International standards

The rights and freedoms that are guaranteed in the ICCPR and ECHR extend to children, including those with mental disability. The UN Convention on the Rights of the Child seeks to eliminate barriers that can prevent children with disabilities from enjoying all these rights. For example, it says:

> "States Parties shall respect and ensure the rights set forth in the present Convention to each child within their jurisdiction without discrimination of any kind, irrespective of the child's... disability, birth or other status." (Article 2)

> "States Parties recognize that a mentally or physically disabled child should enjoy a full and decent life, in conditions which ensure dignity, promote self-reliance and facilitate the child's active participation in the community." (Article 23(1))

On review of the decision to institutionalize a child, the ECHR states:

> "Everyone who is deprived of his liberty... shall be entitled to take proceedings by which the lawfulness of his detention shall be decided speedily by a court and his release ordered if the detention is not lawful." (Article 5(4))

The Convention on the Rights of the Child says:

> "States Parties recognize the right of a child who has been placed by the competent authorities for the purposes of care, protection or treatment of his or her physical or mental health, to a periodic review of the treatment provided to the child and all other circumstances relevant to his or her placement." (Article 25)

On the right to education, Article 2 of Protocol No. 1 to the ECHR states:

> "No person shall be denied the right to education..."

On treatment and conditions for children in institutions, the Convention on the Rights of the Child states:

> "States Parties shall take all appropriate legislative, administrative, social and educational measures to protect the child from all forms of physical or mental violence, injury or abuse, neglect or negligent treatment, maltreatment or exploitation... while in the care of parent(s), legal guardians(s) or any other person who has the care of the child." (Article 19(1))

On separation of children from family, the ICCPR states:

> "No one shall be subjected to arbitrary or unlawful interference with his privacy, family, home or correspondence... Everyone has the right to the protection of the law against such interference or attacks." (Article 17)

The Convention on the Rights of the Child states:

> "The child shall be registered immediately after birth and shall have... as far as possible, the right to know and be cared for by his or her parents." (Article 7(1))

> "States Parties undertake to respect the right of the child to preserve his or her identity, including nationality, name and family relations as recognized by law without unlawful interference." (Article 8(1))

> "States Parties shall ensure that a child shall not be separated from his or her parents against their will, except when competent authorities subject to judicial review determine, in accordance with applicable law and procedures, that such separation is necessary for the best interests of the child." (Article 9(1))

Because their future is regarded as hopeless in the Russian Federation, many human rights are automatically taken away from children with mental disability. Unlike other people who are put in institutions, they are confined only on account of their disability and not because they pose a threat to themselves, or to others, or because their parents are unfit to bring them up. They are consigned to an utterly aimless life – and unlike prisoners they have no chance of review.

Amnesty International questions the legality of the procedures used for institutionalizing these children, which breach many international standards (see box opposite). Above all, the decision to institutionalize such children is taken without reference to any *law* passed by parliament, and without the informed participation of someone to represent the child's best interests. Children caught up in this situation have no legal means of reversing it.

Cruel and degrading institutions

Needs of children with mental disabilities are low down on the priorities for health care in the Russian Federation, and the budget and staffing allocated to the institutions housing them are minimal. The children live in close confinement with little or no sensory stimulation in conditions that are not only cruel, but degrading. Because they are diagnosed as "uneducable", no effort is made to help them become self-sufficient or fulfil their potential. Their treatment shows no respect for the rights of children born with mental disabilities. It also undermines the right of their parents to take responsibility for them.

Over recent decades medical science in many parts of the world has learned more about conditions such as Down's Syndrome and autism, and understood the potential of people who have these conditions. In the Russian Federation, they are classified as "uneducable" in two of the ministerial directives regulating their situation, which date from 1979 and 1986 – before the Russian Federation came into existence.

The Russian Federation has adopted numerous laws on the rights and opportunities of disabled people since it became a sovereign state in 1991, but none relate specifically to the rights of children with mental disability. All of the new laws

Another corridor marked "Beware! Keep Out!" led to a playroom. Three women orderlies stood at the open door of a room approximately 25 square metres in size and painted a cheerful yellow and green. Inside, the room was bare except for a handful of plastic bricks on the floor in one corner. Thirty young people were in the room, crouching by the walls near radiators or rocking on the floor in the middle of the room. The oldest was an 18-year-old man. No one touched the bricks.

A smell of urine was noticeable from the corridor. The orderlies said they spent much of the day cleaning the children as many were incontinent. One complained that she had to do this with her bare hands as the *internat* did not provide the staff with gloves.

Several hours later Amnesty International's delegate returned to the playroom. The same children were there, still in the same places, and the bricks were still untouched.

concern other categories of people, such as the physically disabled who are living at home, or people confined to institutions because of mental illness and violent behaviour.[88] The authorities continue to take an administrative view of children with mental disabilities and to see their problems mainly in terms of budget and staffing. The ministerial directives for dealing with "uneducable" children were updated to this effect in 1997 and 2000.[89] In Amnesty International's view, the situation of these children poses questions of fundamental rights – including the rights to liberty, education, access to justice, and protection from torture and cruel, inhuman or degrading treatment.

Places housing "uneducable" categories of mentally disabled children are known as DDI from their Russian initials (*Detskie doma i internaty* – children's homes and *internats*). The children's homes are run by the Ministry of Health and are intended for children up to the age of four. *Internats* are administered by the Ministry of Labour and Social Development for children up to the age of 18. There are on average two *internats* in each Subject of the Federation with seven in Moscow Region, which is large and densely populated. At the age of 18, people with mental disabilities are placed in neuro-psychological nursing homes run by the Ministry of Labour. Why a child should be transferred from the guardianship of the Ministry of Health to the Ministry of Labour at the age of five – without any reference to his or her state of health – is unclear to Amnesty International. No role is foreseen throughout this process for the Ministry of Education.

Conditions in the DDI are inspected by the procuracy – the state prosecution service. Its role is to ensure that no laws are being broken in the institution. Officials from the State Centre for Sanitary-Epidemiological Inspection also inspect hygiene standards in the DDI. However, there is no provision for regular, detailed and individual reviews of the children to assess their condition with a view to discharge at any point, nor to evaluate the care, treatment or education of the children. At *Internat Z*, one psychologist was working with 205 children. She said that the children receive a thorough assessment at the age of 18, when a visiting commission decides where to place them next.

The number of *internats* has fallen slightly. In its third draft report to the UN Committee on the Rights of the Child, the Russian Federation said that in 2001 there were 155 *internats*. In its second report, it said it had 157 DDI for disabled children in 1996. It said these 157 DDI had:

> *"30,700 residents suffering from various forms of mental backwardness and physical ailments, who could not be kept by their parents under domestic conditions, or orphans whose physical and mental health was seriously impaired. Of the 30,700 children in these boarding institutions, 5,600 are permanently confined to their beds".*[90]

The second report did not indicate how many of the residents had been born with mental disability and removed from their parents. However, in an earlier report to the Committee on the Rights of the Child in 1993, the Russian Federation said that children with mental disability accounted for more than half the total number of *internat* inmates in 1991.[91]

Ministerial directives for putting children with mental disability in DDI also determine their conditions inside.[92] In children's homes, on a 24-hour rota two duty nurses are assigned to 100 children, with an additional nurse to handle 50 children who are bed-bound.[93] The directives state that ward orderlies should deal with the children's moment-to-moment needs. This function, however, is not listed in their job descriptions, drawn up and confirmed in 1995 by the Ministries of Labour and Social Development and by the State Committee of Higher Education.[94] These say that it is the orderlies' job to clean premises to a hygienic standard; to assist the nurse in dispensing medication; to receive, store and dispense laundry and domestic equipment; and to tidy the bedside tables of bed-bound patients after each meal.

In *internats* for children aged between five and 18, the ratio of staff to children is lower, with 250 children in the care of one doctor. Nursing staff at *Internat Z* told Amnesty International that their monthly pay was 1,000 roubles — roughly equivalent to US$30. Section IV of the 1979 Directive states that no effort is to be made to teach or train "uneducable" children.

New attitudes, old practices

In recent years the authorities have begun to acknowledge the woeful way that children with mental disability in the Russian Federation are treated. However, to date they have not taken the steps necessary to remedy the problem.

A 1998 State Report, *On the Situation of Children in the Russian Federation*, acknowledged, "Some categories of children, considered to be uneducable, are very often placed in Ministry of Labour institutions where they do not receive the development they need and are placed beyond the margins of the educational system."[95] The report criticized the level of medical and social care available to them.[96]

This forthrightness was echoed in a television program, *Hero of the Day*, broadcast on Russian television's *Channel Four* on 29 June 2000. The then Vice-Premier Valentina Matvienko told the program, "Previously we used to 'write off' children with disabilities and off-load them onto the *internats* — something that in fact even exacerbated their disability."

Although frank, neither government statement heralded a new approach towards these children.

The federal parliamentary ombudsman's 2001 report on the rights and opportunities of disabled people (see above) identified social stigma as the main obstacle facing "invalids". It catalogued different efforts made to help them since the adoption of the 1995

Law on the Social Protection of Invalids. It concluded that the efforts fell short because they did not reflect what "invalids" need, but what donors would give.[97] He called for a new "rights-based" approach and a federal law — on the rights of the disabled — that would prohibit discrimination against disabled people of any sort on the grounds of their disability. As far as Amnesty International is aware, by January 2003 the State *Duma* had taken no action on this recommendation.

In 2002 the parliamentary ombudsman for Moscow Region published a S*pecial Thematic Report on the Rights of the Child*. This noted, "Children's homes and *internats* are not fulfilling their primary function — which is to help children adapt to normal life." He concluded with a recommendation to the Moscow Regional *Duma* to legislate for setting up a system of foster families for children whose parents did not want to bring them up — modelled on a network of 1,000 foster families in Samara region which the report praised.[98]

The UN Committee on the Rights of the Child also made recommendations to the Russian Federation when considering its two periodic reports on implementing the Convention on the Rights of the Child in 1993 and 1999. In 1993 it "recognize[d] the legacy of certain attitudes which hamper the implementation of the rights of the child. These relate to, *inter alia*, the institutionalization of child care, the disabled and family responsibilities."[99] It urged the Russian Federation to set up a National State Committee to coordinate and monitor implementation of the Convention.[100]

In 1999, the Committee expressed its serious concern at the scale of institutionalization of children in the Russian Federation and the conditions in which institutionalized children live.[101] It recommended the authorities adopt appropriate procedures "to provide for the periodic review of all types of placement" and reform of the inspection system "in particular by reinforcing the role and power of independent inspection mechanisms and ensuring their right to inspect foster homes and public institutions without warning".[102]

The Committee expressed special concern about the plight of "children with mental disabilities and children living in institutions", and in particular the "current diagnosis system and practices" and the "conditions for disabled children living in institutions."[103] The Russian Federation was due to report to the Committee for a third time in 2002. In its draft report which Amnesty International has seen, it says it has set up an Inter-Agency Co-ordinating Committee on the rights of the child, and has improved inspections of institutions through the establishment of Children's Ombudsmen in 15 Subjects of the Russian Federation, including the Chechen Republic. Amnesty International has not been able to access reports issued by any of these Children's Ombudsmen. The government's draft report does not address the question of ensuring systematic review of placements, recommended by the UN Committee.

The newspaper *Nezavisimaia gazeta* carried a rare article on children with Down's Syndrome on 24 July 2002. It said that in Russia:

> *"... a Down's [Syndrome] baby is whisked away immediately after birth without being shown to the mother. It is explained to the parents that caring for and raising such a child is very hard work, and that because of the enormous number of possible problems with internal organs (heart disease, impaired pancreatic function etc...) such children generally don't live to see 25...*
>
> *"The child is sent first to an infants' home and later to an* internat *for disabled children. Once a Down's [Syndrome] child ends up there, he or she will never learn to relate to other people... The* internat *staff simply won't be able to devote enough time to the youngster. They won't even try to teach him to talk, dress himself or eat with a spoon. If he starts hitting his head against the wall, they'll tie him to his bed. He will remain at the level of a vegetable and most likely won't live to adulthood...*
>
> *"In other countries, thanks to rehabilitative measures, people with Down's Syndrome have lived as long as 60 years and have got not only a secondary education but even higher schooling... In Russia the majority of Down's [Syndrome] sufferers don't even get an elementary education..."*

Amnesty International is concerned that children with mental disabilities in the Russian Federation are being deprived of their right to liberty by unfair procedures. They are losing their right to an education and their right to a family life, and living in institutional conditions that do not respect their inherent dignity.

As a basic minimum, Amnesty International believes that the Russian Federation should adopt a law, whose primary concern is the best interests of children with mental disability. This should set down the procedures and criteria for placing a child in an institution and taking him or her away from their family. The child's best interests should be represented by an appropriate independent expert, who seeks the child's view and, where possible, articulates it and intervenes in his or her best interest. An independent and impartial court should review the substance of all such decisions.

This law should guarantee that the placement is automatically subject to a systematic and regular review, and where continued institutionalization is shown to be in the best interests of the child, should prescribe conditions for the treatment and welfare of the child. It should be drafted in consultation with qualified experts, the parents of children with mental disability, and with non-governmental organizations working in the field of mental disability.

Chapter 7: Prisoners unprotected

It is a struggle to get justice in the Russian Federation, but for prisoners the struggle can be even harder. The 2002 Punishment-Implementation Code did expand the opportunities available to prisoners. Formally, these now include access to the courts, to the Federal Human Rights Commissioner, and to international human rights bodies, once domestic remedies have been exhausted.[104] For prisoners in certain circumstances, however, these are not effective remedies. This chapter focuses on prisoners whose rights were violated by riot squads deployed in the penitentiary system, and on prisoners serving life sentences.

Abuse by riot squads

Since 1998 the Ministry of Justice has been responsible for administering the penitentiary system in the Russian Federation. Nevertheless, it has left the control of prison disorders in the hands of riot squads who are outside the prison system and not answerable to it. By abdicating from its responsibility for this aspect of prison management, the Ministry of Justice may be putting unarmed prisoners at risk of extreme, random and gratuitous violence. The remedies available to prisoners are too limited and too ineffective to redress effectively such violation of their human rights.

The following example of ill-treatment by a riot squad is from Perm Region in the Ural mountains. It took place in the men's ordinary regime corrective labour colony AM-244/9-11 in Chepets settlement, Cherdyn district. Although some aspects of the case were disputed, the following basic facts emerged uncontested by either party during a hearing before Cherdyn District Court from 4 to 8 February 2002.

- On 17 April 2001 members of the Detachment of Special Police (known as OMON)[105] of the regional Department of Internal Affairs were summoned from Perm to the colony in Chepets. Seven masked OMON members entered the punishment cells and the strict regime barracks in the colony. They called out the prisoners and beat them in the corridors, using truncheons, feet and fists. The seven men wore no identifying badges. This process was repeated until 20 April. Three prisoners suffered broken ribs.

- Prisoners in other barracks were called to the drill ground and made to undress or jump over poles, and were beaten with fists and kicked when they failed to do so. In the canteen some prisoners were hit without warning from behind by OMON members wielding truncheons. Around 140 prisoners wrote statements saying they had suffered some form of assault.

- On 9 June 2001, a month after the Perm Regional Ombudsman had launched a commission to investigate the incident, the procurator of Cherdyn district brought a criminal case "for illegal use of special techniques" against the OMON.[106] He had at first refused to investigate the prisoners' complaints.

At the trial, the charge of "illegal use of special techniques" against the OMON was dropped because the prisoners could not identify the officers concerned as they had been wearing masks at the time of the alleged beatings. A lesser offence of "negligence" was brought against their commander, S.L. Bromberg, of which he was acquitted. The procuracy challenged the acquittal before the Perm Regional Court, which in May 2002 ordered a retrial on procedural grounds. At the time of preparing this report, the retrial had not taken place.

Much of the original dispute at the trial revolved around whether the OMON troops had made legitimate demands of the prisoners in Chepets, which the prisoners had disobeyed. In Amnesty International's view, other fundamental questions of penal policy are also raised in this case.

The OMON were set up within the Ministry of Internal Affairs of the USSR by an internal regulation of 3 October 1989. Their purpose was to preserve public order (at large public events or at times of catastrophe and epidemic), prevent mass unrest, and help detain armed criminals.

The OMON were not an integral part of the Soviet prison administration and were not envisaged as such. They were

International standards

The Basic Principles for the Treatment of Prisoners, Principle 4, states:

> "The responsibility of prisons for the custody of prisoners and for the protection of society against crime shall be discharged in keeping with a State's other social objectives and its fundamental responsibilities for promoting the well-being and development of all members of society."

The Standard Minimum Rules for the Treatment of Prisoners state:

> "Discipline and order shall be maintained with firmness, but with no more restriction than is necessary for safe custody and well-ordered community life."
> (Rule 27)

> "Officers of the institutions shall not, in their relations with the prisoners, use force except in self-defence or in cases of attempted escape, or active or passive physical resistance to an order based on law or regulations. Officers who have recourse to force must use no more than is strictly necessary and must report the incident immediately to the director of the institution." (Rule 54(1))

The Basic Principles on the Use of Force and Firearms by Law Enforcement Officials, Principle 15, states:

> "Law enforcement officials, in their relations with persons in custody or detention, shall not use force, except when strictly necessary for the maintenance of security and order within the institution, or when personal safety is threatened."

Recommendation No. R (82) 17 on Custody and Treatment of Dangerous Prisoners, of the Committee of Ministers of the Council of Europe, states:

> "1. To apply, as far as possible, ordinary prison regulations to dangerous prisoners;
> 2. To apply security measures only to the extent to which they are necessarily required;
> 3. To apply security measures in a way respectful of human dignity and rights;
> 4. To ensure that security measures take into account the varying requirements of different kinds of dangerousness;
> 5. To counteract, to the extent feasible, the possible adverse effects of reinforced security conditions;
> 6. To devote all necessary attention to the health problems which might result from reinforced security;
> ...
> 10. To provide suitable training and information for all staff concerned with the custody and treatment of dangerous prisoners."

OMON (special police detachments) forces line up ready for action in Chechnya, July 2001. After a tour of duty in Chechnya they may be recalled to keep order in the prison service elsewhere in the Russian Federation. It was masked troops such as these who were deployed against unarmed prisoners in Chepets colony AM-244/9-11 in April 2001.

available for redeployment within the penitentiary system when judged necessary by the Ministry of Internal Affairs, which at that time was responsible for the administration of the penitentiary system. Since this responsibility passed to the Ministry of Justice in 1998, even this debatable rationale no longer applies.

The OMON unit deployed to Chepets used the nickname "Variag" — or Varangians — which was the name of Scandinavian mercenaries hired in early Russia to force outlying people into submission.[107] During the court hearing in February 2002, it emerged that the "Variag" had just returned from active military combat in Chechnya before its deployment to the colony in Chepets. By the time the trial took place, one of its members was not available to testify because he had gone back on a tour of duty in Chechnya. In Amnesty International's view, the ethos and preparation of these troops was totally inappropriate for dealing with unarmed prisoners in a civilian setting.

In all the accounts of the episode, prisoners whom the OMON targeted were already in punishment cells or secure barracks, and then called outside to be beaten, kicked and

A case brought before the European Court of Human Rights in December 2001, although brought on a separate issue, made reference to another case of ill-treatment by OMON troops, this time against detainees awaiting trial in prison IZ-47/1, Magadan region, on the northeast shore of the Russian Federation, in 1996.

Valerii Kalashnikov, who brought his case on issues relating to his conditions and length of detention, was in the Magadan prison when OMON troops were deployed there in July 1996 and reportedly ill-treated detainees. He received no assistance afterwards from the prison doctor or from the regional procuracy. Having failed to get redress through means available to him locally, he brought a successful complaint to the European Court of Human Rights, which awarded him €5,000 compensation plus €3,000 for costs and expenses.[108]

According to a summary of this part of his complaint, on 15 July 1996 OMON forces used physical force when inmates resisted during a search of cells. Valerii Kalashnikov complained that for several days the OMON forces "beat inmates, including himself, with rubber truncheons, kicked them, made them run through the corridors and spread-eagled them against the wall".

Valerii Kalashnikov spent four years and two months in custody from June 1995 awaiting trial on a charge of embezzlement.

punched. There is no suggestion — even by OMON members — that a prison disturbance was in progress. A prisoner testified that the Chepets administration had called in the OMON because of a dispute with one prisoner, who had refused to obey an order. The prisoner, known as "The North", was used to keep other inmates in order.

The role of prison staff during the incident at the Chepets colony also raises concerns. According to several prisoners, duty staff and the Head of Security reportedly pointed out specific prisoners for the OMON unit to target, whether or not they were offering resistance at the time. Because the prison doctor was married to the deputy security chief, many prisoners who said they had been hurt by the OMON did not register their injuries with her because they feared repercussions from her husband if they did so. One prisoner who visited the doctor alleged that she told him that she had instructions not to register injuries inflicted by the OMON.

Prisoners' requests to have an independent medical examination were turned down by the Cherdyn District Court, according to an eyewitness account of the trial. The Court also

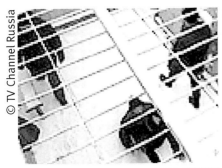

© TV Channel Russia

Steel-plated exercise area (above) and a prisoner receiving food in his cell, Fire Island.

rejected their request to call witnesses and to provide the prisoners with lawyers.

Amnesty International is concerned that prisoners at Chepets colony were ill-treated by OMON troops and have had no effective redress and compensation. The organization urges the federal authorities to ensure that personnel used to maintain order are trained to abide by international standards, and that all prisoners have access to effective remedies if their human rights are violated.

Life imprisonment

Conditions for prisoners serving life sentences in the Russian Federation are so harsh that they amount to cruel, inhuman or degrading treatment or punishment, and in some cases possibly even torture.

Life imprisonment is a new punishment in the Russian Federation and is best understood in the context of the death penalty debate that divided the country in the 1990s.

Although obliged to abolish the death penalty since the Russian Federation joined the Council of Europe in 1996, the State *Duma* has failed to do so. Reluctantly, it introduced an alternative punishment to death – life imprisonment, which the authorities have made as harsh as possible.

In 1996 the then President, Boris Yeltsin, issued a decree commuting all existing death sentences to terms of imprisonment. Courts, however, continued to pass death sentences and prisoners accumulated on death row. In February 1999 the Constitutional Court ruled that the death penalty was unconstitutional in the absence of a nationwide jury system to hear capital cases. Courts then stopped sentencing prisoners to death and in July 1999 a further presidential decree commuted to terms of imprisonment the death sentences of the 716 prisoners who were on death row.

It was against this background that life imprisonment was introduced in the 1996 Criminal Code for especially grave crimes, when a court "considers it is impossible to impose a death sentence".[109] People previously ineligible for a death sentence under Russian law – women, and men aged 65 and over or under 18 at the time of the crime – also cannot be sentenced to imprisonment for life.

The new Criminal Code increased the length of sentences available for "especially grave crimes". In the Soviet era, a maximum penalty of 15 years' imprisonment was the alternative to a death sentence, and death penalties could be commuted to 20 years' imprisonment. The 1996 Criminal Code introduced harsher alternatives to the death penalty: 25 years' imprisonment, or imprisonment for life.

Five crimes now carry a possible sentence of life imprisonment, all of them defined as "especially grave". They are:

- murder in aggravated circumstances;
- an attempt on the life of a state or public official (described as "terrorism");
- an attempt on the life of someone investigating a crime or carrying out justice;
- an attempt on the life of a law enforcement officer;
- genocide.[110]

Life imprisonment means imprisonment for the duration of a prisoner's natural life. Contrary to international standards for the treatment of people in custody, in the Russian Federation life imprisonment is organized around the prisoner's almost total isolation. This isolation, along with other hardships, leads Amnesty International to believe that their rights under Articles 7 and 10 of the ICCPR are being violated.

Life sentence prisoners serve their time on "special regime", which is the harshest category of imprisonment in the system of corrective labour colonies. According to the 1997 Punishment-Implementation Code, they are kept separately from other "special regime" prisoners, who serve their sentences in barracks.[111]

Every aspect of imprisonment for prisoners serving life sentences is designed to ensure their isolation from the outside world and from other prisoners. They are held in cells,

'High security risk prisoners'

The European Committee for the Prevention of Torture (CPT) has published a series of "Substantive Statements" on conditions for different categories of prisoner. On "high security risk prisoners", it stated:

"This group of prisoners will (or at least should, if the classification system is operating satisfactorily) represent a very small proportion of the overall prison population. However it is a group that is of particular concern to the CPT, as the need to take exceptional measures vis-à-vis such prisoners brings with it a greater risk of inhuman treatment.

"Prisoners who represent a particularly high security risk should, within the confines of their detention units, enjoy a relatively relaxed regime by way of compensation for their severe custodial situation. In particular they should be able to meet their fellow prisoners in the unit and be granted a good deal of choice about activities. Special efforts should be made to develop a good internal atmosphere within high-security units... The existence of a satisfactory programme of activities is just as important – if not more so – in a high security unit than on normal location."[12]

The CPT was established by the European Convention for the Prevention of Torture and Inhuman or Degrading Treatment or Punishment, which the Russian Federation ratified in 1998.

either alone or in the company of one other prisoner. They exercise in a separate enclosed yard outside their cell for 90 minutes each day, and are given work assignments to do inside a separate workshop.[13] They are entitled to study, but may not take part in education classes with other prisoners, studying instead in their cells on their own.[14] Life sentence prisoners are entitled in principle to have only a three-hour visit twice a year and to receive one parcel and one small package a year. The money they earn on work assignments can be spent each month on items from the prison kiosk.[15]

The provisions isolating life sentence prisoners contravene those recommended by international standards, and the way they are put into practice makes them even harsher.

The sudden influx of prisoners sentenced to terms on "special regime" since executions stopped in 1996 put pressure on the places available and prompted the authorities to open new institutions. One is institution OE 265/5, housed in a converted monastery on an island in White Lake in Vologda region, between Moscow and Arkhangelsk in the northwest of the country. It is called "Fire Island" by local people who can see the prison lights across the lake. It accommodates 156 people with commuted death sentences, according to statistics provided by the Ministry of Justice to a delegation of State *Duma* deputies visiting the prison in February 2002. Since the first prisoner arrived in the colony in February 1994, the Ministry reports that 32 prisoners have died, four of whom committed suicide. This is a mortality rate of around 20 per cent in six years.

Opponents of abolishing the death penalty have used figures like these to argue that execution is more humane than what they call the "slow death" of life imprisonment. In Amnesty International's view, the figures indicate that the conditions in which life sentence prisoners are held violate their right to be treated with humanity and not to be subjected to torture or other cruel, inhuman or degrading treatment – and that the conditions should be improved without delay.

Journalist Anna Komia described "Fire Island" in the newspaper *Vremia MN* on 12 February 2002:

> *"The colony has 81 cells, 20 of them two-person shop cells where the prisoners exercise their right to work. They sew industrial gloves, earning 25 roubles a day. The living cells also house two men each, or sometimes three, but the latter is only a temporary arrangement.*

> *"A prisoner may leave his cell only in the presence of a duty officer and three other guards. They leave their cells only to go to work, visit the bathhouse or take exercise (an hour and a half in a steel-plated box measuring three by four metres)... Prisoners are permitted to buy television sets, but only 15 men in the entire colony have been able to do so. Each cell does have a radio, though: it is used to broadcast edifying and educational talks. The menu is based on expenditure of 22 roubles 50 kopecks [about US$0.70] a day..."*

According to some of the letters that prisoners have managed to send from the island, even this picture does not match reality. Work is not always available, so prisoners without work have no way of occupying their time and have no source of income with which to buy essentials such as soap, toothpaste, shaving tools and envelopes.

Prisoners serving life sentences face major difficulties in maintaining contact with loved ones, especially given the enormous size of the Russian Federation and the severe limitations placed on the frequency and length of visits. Whereas prisoners sentenced to milder regimes are sent to colonies in their home region, this provision does not apply to prisoners on "special regime", according to Article 73(3) of the Punishment-Implementation Code.

There are currently five institutions for prisoners serving life sentences in the Russian Federation: the one in Vologda Region mentioned above and others in Perm and Sverdlovsk Regions (in the Ural mountains area) and in Mordovia and Orenburg (in the central zone).[116] A prisoner from one of the other 84 Subjects of the Federation might find himself several thousand kilometres away from home — and even several time zones away from his relatives. For instance, a prisoner from Chukhotka Region on the northeast coast serving a life sentence in the nearest "special regime" colony in Sverdlovsk Region, would be nine time zones away from home. Such distances can mean life sentence prisoners have no personal contact, since not every family can afford the time or expense of such a long journey. In the *Vremia MN* article, the journalist noted that out of 156 inmates, only 40 "maintain contact" with relatives, which could amount to just one letter a year.

This imposes extreme physical and psychological isolation on life sentence prisoners and also makes them utterly dependent on the fairness and professionalism of the people administering their punishment. If this professionalism is missing, the prisoner's only direct channel for redress is writing to the procuracy, which is responsible for ensuring that legality is observed in the region, or to the regional ombudsman, if there is one. At the time of writing this report, regional ombudsmen were operating in Perm and Sverdlovsk

Deaths of Chechen prisoners

Salman Raduev was sentenced to life imprisonment in November 2001 by the Dagestan Supreme Court for masterminding the taking of hostages in Kizliar in 1996. He died on 14 December 2002, aged 36, reportedly in the therapy wing of the Perm "special regime" colony – the "special regime" institution nearest to the Chechen Republic. On 17 December the Ministry of Justice stated that a post-mortem revealed that, "he died of natural causes as a result of massive internal haemorrhaging". The possible cause of the haemorrhaging was not suggested. The report said he had suffered a bloodshot eye from 6 December and made no complaints about his medical treatment. He was interred in a municipal cemetery in Perm Region on 18 December 2002 with no relatives present.[117] As Salman Raduev's death was "from natural causes", the report said, the procuracy had decided not to investigate it.

On 27 November Salman Raduev had been visited by federal investigators from Moscow, wanting information about Akhmed Zakayev, whom the authorities were trying to extradite from Denmark. Akhmed Zakayev is the representative abroad of the Chechen President Aslan Maskhadov. Denmark refused to extradite him. The federal investigator interrogated Salman Raduev without anyone else present. The lawyer for the Raduev family says that they received no notification of his death. The Ministry of Justice claims that it sent written notification to them, and that when the family did not respond within three days, the Ministry arranged his burial without them.

Salman Raduev died barely four months after his co-defendant **Turpal-Ali Atgeriev,** former Deputy Prime Minister of the Chechen Republic. Turpal-Ali Atgeriev was serving a 15-year prison sentence when he died on 20 August 2002, five months after his trial. The Ministry of Justice reported that he died from leukaemia. His relatives received no information about his illness, death or burial.

Amnesty International urges the authorities to initiate an independent investigation into the circumstances in which these two men died. It should be conducted by people chosen for their recognized competence, expertise and independence, who would command authority and inspire confidence. Adequate financial, human and technical resources must be guaranteed. The investigation should have the power to compel the disclosure of documents, the attendance of witnesses, and obtain all the information necessary to it. Its mandate should include the power to make findings on the manner and cause of death, identify anyone reasonably suspected of responsibility, and make recommendations aimed at minimizing the risk of deaths by other than natural causes in custody in the future. The scope, methods and findings of the investigation should be made public.

© AFP/Getty Images

Salman Raduev

but had not been appointed in Vologda, Mordovia and Orenburg.

Those convicted of "terrorism" in connection with the conflict in Chechnya may be particularly vulnerable to ill-treatment in custody, particularly while the fighting continues or when other incidents, such as the October 2002 hostage-taking in Moscow, result in a backlash against Chechens in society at large.

Both the Chechen prisoners described in the box opposite had begun long sentences in "special regime" colony VK-240/3-14 in Perm Region when they died in 2002, only months after their trial. There was no independent investigation into their deaths, and their families were not kept fully informed about their autopsies and burials, or the events leading up to their deaths. Although the Ministry of Justice has posted some information on its website to meet media interest at home and abroad, it has done nothing to allay their families' suspicion that they did not die of natural causes.

As yet there are no centralized rules on the day-to-day requirements of prisoners on "special regime", which allows colony directors too much leeway. Parliamentarians and human rights activists who have visited these colonies describe regimes that are needlessly restrictive in some places and downright humiliating in others. Life sentence prisoners in Perm, Vologda and Mordovia for instance, are handcuffed each time they are moved from their cell, no matter who the prisoner is or how short the distance. Life sentence prisoners in Mordovia are made to adopt a special walk in front of prison staff, with bowed heads and small steps. The purpose of this treatment is not clear. Amnesty International believes that rules that conform to international standards should be adopted and implemented as soon as possible.

Like all convicted people in the Russian Federation, prisoners with life sentences have a constitutional right to petition the President for clemency.[118] Their opportunities for a judicial review of their sentence are not clear. Within one

International standards

Article 3(1) of the Punishment-Implementation Code states that, "wherever financial and social conditions permit" international standards will be applied and take precedence in the penal system. This disclaimer contradicts Article 15(4) of the Russian Federation's Constitution, which states that international standards are part of domestic law, and always take precedence over it in cases of discrepancy.

Article 7 of the ICCPR states:

"No one shall be subjected to torture or to cruel, inhuman or degrading treatment or punishment."

Article 10 of the ICCPR states:

"(1) All persons deprived of their liberty shall be treated with humanity and with respect for the inherent dignity of the human person.

"(3) The penitentiary system shall comprise treatment of prisoners the essential aim of which shall be their reformation and social rehabilitation."

On solitary confinement, the Basic Principles for the Treatment of Prisoners, Principle 7, states:

"Efforts addressed to the abolition of solitary confinement as a punishment, or to the restriction of its use, should be undertaken and encouraged."

The European Prison Rules state:

"Punishment by disciplinary confinement ... shall only be imposed if the medical officer after examination certifies in writing that the prisoner is fit to sustain it." (Rule 38(1))

"The medical officer shall visit daily prisoners undergoing such punishments and shall advise the director if the termination or alteration of the punishment is considered necessary on grounds of physical or mental health." (Rule 38(3))

The 2nd General Report on the European Committee for the Prevention of Torture's Activities stated:

"Solitary confinement can, in certain circumstances, amount to inhuman and degrading treatment; in any event, all forms of solitary confinement should be as short as possible." (Paragraph 56)

On contact with family, Article 8 of the ECHR states:

"Everyone has the right to respect for his private and family life..."

The Body of Principles for the Protection of All Persons under Any Form of Detention or Imprisonment, states:

"A detained or imprisoned person shall have the right to be visited by and to correspond with, in particular, members of his family and shall be given adequate opportunity to communicate with the outside world, subject to reasonable conditions and restrictions as specified by law or lawful regulations." (Principle 19)

"If a detained or imprisoned person so requests, he shall if possible be kept in a place of detention or imprisonment reasonably near his usual place of residence." (Principle 20)

On other contact with the outside world, the Standard Minimum Rules for the Treatment of Prisoners, Rule 39, states:

"Prisoners shall be kept informed regularly of the more important items of news by the reading of newspapers, periodicals or special institutional publications, by hearing wireless transmissions, by lectures or by any similar means as authorized or controlled by the administration."

On prisoners' remedies, the International Covenant on Civil and Political Rights, Article 2(3), states:

Each State Party to the present Covenant undertakes:

(a) To ensure that any person whose rights or freedoms as herein recognized are violated shall have an effective remedy, notwithstanding that the violation has been committed by persons acting in an official capacity;

(b) To ensure that any persons claiming such a remedy shall have his right thereto determined by competent judicial, administrative or legislative authorities, or by any other competent authority provided for by the legal system of the State, and to develop the possibilities of judicial remedy;

(c) To ensure that the competent authorities shall enforce such remedies when granted.

The European Convention on Human Rights, Article 13, states:

"Everyone whose rights and freedoms as set forth in this Convention are violated shall have an effective remedy before a national authority notwithstanding that the violation has been committed by persons acting in an official capacity."

The Body of Principles for the Protection of All Persons under Any Form of Detention or Imprisonment, Principle 33, states:

"(1) A detained or imprisoned person or his counsel shall have the right to make a request or complaint regarding his treatment, in particular in case of torture or other cruel, inhuman or degrading treatment, to the authorities responsible for the administration of the place of detention and to higher authorities and, when necessary, to appropriate authorities vested with reviewing or remedial powers.

"(4) Every request or complaint shall be promptly dealt with and replied to without undue delay. If the request or complaint is rejected or, in cases of inordinate delay, the complainant shall be entitled to bring it before a judicial, or other authority. Neither the detained or imprisoned person nor any complainant under paragraph 1 of the present principle shall suffer prejudice for making a request or complaint."

The Standard Minimum Rules for the Treatment of Prisoners, Rule 36, states:

"It shall be possible to make requests or complaints to the inspector of prisons during his inspection. The prisoner shall have the opportunity to talk to the inspector or to any other inspecting officer without the director or other members of the staff being present." (Rule 36(2))

"Every prisoner shall be allowed to make a request or complaint, without censorship as to the substance but in proper form, to the central prison administration, the judicial authority or other proper authorities through approved channels." (Rule 36(3))

On review of sentence, the European Court of Human Rights, in the case of *Hussain v the United Kingdom* in 1996, elaborated on the need for judicial review of sentences. Abed Hussain had been convicted of murder at the age of 16 and given a discretionary life sentence at Her Majesty's Pleasure. The Court found that without adequate and regular opportunity for judicial review:

"A young person could be found to have forfeited his liberty all his life, which raises questions under Article 3 of the ECHR."[119]

Judicial review should take the form,

"...of an oral hearing in the context of adversarial procedure, involving legal representation and the possibility of calling and questioning witnesses."[120]

month of a prisoner completing a statutory part of his sentence, the administration of the colony is obliged to consider submitting a request for early release to a court on his behalf.[121] For a prisoner with a life sentence, an application may be submitted only if he has had no disciplinary infractions for the previous three years.[122] Should the colony administration decide to apply, and their application be turned down, a new application for a court hearing cannot be submitted for a further three years.[123] The Code does not state what constitutes the "statutory part" of a life sentence.

According to the Clemency Department of the Presidential Administration, prisoners submitted more than 6,600 petitions for clemency during 2002, of which 181 were granted by President Putin.[124] It is not known how many of these – if any – were submitted by prisoners serving life imprisonment. These statistics are kept by the Ministry of Justice and are not publicly available.

Regional clemency commissions in areas with a dense prison population, such as Mordovia, Orenburg, Perm, Sverdlovsk and Vologda, each processed among the highest number of petitions for the year of 2002, according to statistics from the federal clemency department. The commissions are new and each has a different way of working.[125] The commission in Orenburg, for instance, met nine times but never visited a corrective labour colony. In Sverdlovsk, one of the commission's 11 meetings took place inside colony walls. The number of recommendations for pardon also varied and may have been based on differing criteria. These ranged from one recommendation for pardon out of every four petitions received in Sverdlovsk Region, to one in every 82 in Perm Region.

Since life imprisonment is a relatively new form of punishment in the Russian Federation, Amnesty International urges the authorities to reassess its aims and the way it is currently being applied. Among other things, life sentence prisoners should have many more opportunities for social contact. They should also have the possibility of a judicial review of their sentence within a reasonable period.

At this stage of the Russian Federation's penal history, Amnesty International believes that all life sentences passed

Regional clemency commission figures			
Federal Subject	Prisoners in 2002	Petitions received in 2002	Recommendations for pardon in 2002
Republic of Mordovia	17,313	80	10
Vologda Region	No statistics	181	18
Sverdlovsk Region	48,450	341	82
Orenburg Region	15,220	141	20
Perm Region	36,003	329	4

before 1 January 2002 should be reviewed, as the proceedings underlying the convictions were conducted under the old CPC, which has been substantially amended because of its lack of conformity with international fair trial standards.[126]

While a custodial alternative to executions is welcome, Amnesty International urges the Russian Federation, as a matter of urgency, to ensure that people convicted of serious crimes are guaranteed treatment that respects their rights and complies with human rights standards.

Chapter 8: Recommendations

Amnesty International believes that the following measures would radically improve the protection of human rights in the Russian Federation.

On international human rights standards

The Russian Federation should ensure respect and implementation of all relevant international human rights standards in order to ensure that all those living on its territory enjoy access to justice, including through:

- Withdrawing the reservations made to Article 5(3) and 5(4) — which relate to procedures for arrest and detention — when it ratified the European Convention on Human Rights (ECHR).
- Tabling before the State *Duma* and adopting without delay laws on introducing a moratorium on the death penalty and authorizing ratification of Protocol No. 6 to the ECHR. The Russian Federation should also prepare for the speedy ratification of the Second Optional Protocol to the International Covenant on Civil and Political Rights, aiming at the abolition of the death penalty, and Protocol No. 13 to the ECHR, that abolish the death penalty for crimes committed during times of war as well as peace.
- Authorizing immediately the publication of the full reports and recommendations made by the European Committee for the Prevention of Torture and Inhuman or Degrading Treatment or Punishment (CPT) on its visits to the Russian Federation. The material should be accessible to the general public and the specialist press. The Russian Federation should also set up a steering group within the presidential administration to ensure that the Committee's recommendations are put into effect.
- Ensuring that no one is extradited to any country where they will be at risk of the death penalty, torture or proceedings that fail to meet international fair trial standards.

On upholding and promoting respect for the law

The Russian Federation should ensure that the justice system is fully respected in order to protect rights and combat impunity, and

that non-judicial mechanisms for the protection of human rights
are empowered to promote accountability, including through:

- Ensuring that the presumption of innocence of all people
  suspected of, or charged with, a criminal offence is
  respected, unless and until they have been found guilty
  after a fair trial. Practices that may have an impact on the
  presumption of innocence – such as shaving the head of
  male suspects and placing the accused in a cage in a
  courtroom – should be discontinued. Extra security
  measures should only be taken when there is a
  demonstrable risk that the suspect poses a danger or is
  liable to escape.
- Ensuring that the relevant bodies initiate proceedings
  against anyone who defies rulings of the Constitutional
  Court on the registration of residence. President Putin in
  particular should use all political and legal measures
  available to him to ensure that rulings of the Constitutional
  Court are obeyed.
- Amending the 1998 Law on Combating Terrorism to
  establish clear operational lines of accountability in "anti-
  terrorist" operations. The Russian Federation authorities
  should ensure that anyone responsible for violating human
  rights in the context of "anti-terrorist" operations is
  brought to justice in proceedings that meet international
  standards of fairness, as recommended in the Council of
  Europe's Expert Opinion. They should also guarantee that
  victims receive adequate reparation.
- Reminding anyone involved in "anti-terrorist" operations –
  law enforcement agencies, members of the security forces
  and government officials, including the President – that
  their actions must be carried out in accordance with
  internationally accepted standards on the use of force and
  respect for the rights of suspects and victims.
- Adopting a federal law for the regional ombudsman
  institution that is grounded in Article 2 of the Constitution
  and includes a general mandate for their work that can be
  expanded but not reduced by regional legislatures.
- The State *Duma* and parliaments in each of the Subjects of
  the Federation with an ombudsman should ensure that he

or she can carry out their work, and make provisions —
including financial provision — to ensure the speedy
implementation of the ombudsman's recommendations.

On protection and redress for vulnerable groups

The Russian Federation should ensure that those who are
particularly vulnerable to abuses of their rights, such as
children born with mental disability and prisoners, are
afforded protection and redress, including through:

- Ratifying Protocol No. 12 to the ECHR, which sets out a
  general prohibition of discrimination.
- The State *Duma* should act on the recommendation of the
  Federal Human Rights Commissioner in his 2001 *Report on
  the Rights and Opportunities of the Disabled*, which called
  for the adoption of a law that defines the legal rights of
  disabled people and prohibits discrimination against them.
- The State *Duma* should adopt legislation that prescribes, at
  a minimum, the criteria and procedures for separating a
  child from their family and placing them in an institution,
  and guarantees them automatic, systematic periodic review
  of their placement, treatment and welfare. Such a law
  should be drafted in consultation with qualified experts,
  including non-governmental organizations, and with input
  from parents. It should provide that the best interest of the
  child is the primary concern; that the child should at all
  times be represented by an independent and appropriate
  expert who seeks their views (if possible) and intervenes in
  their best interest; and that the substance of all such
  decisions is subject to review by a qualified independent
  and impartial court.
- Courts established under the new Juvenile Justice System
  should have responsibility for adjudicating placements of
  children with mental disability in institutions, after
  soliciting informed opinion from all relevant parties to
  determine the best interest of the child. These placements
  should be the subject of regular, periodic judicial reviews
  that entail a detailed individual case history from the
  institution, and include a record of the efforts invested to
  prepare the child to be as self-sufficient as possible. On the

basis of this information, testimony from relatives and, where appropriate, interviews with the child, the court should decide on whether or not the child should be reintegrated into the community.

- The Ministries of Health, Labour and Social Welfare should compile detailed statistics on the children with mental disability in their care, and place them in the public domain.
- The administration of institutions dealing with children with mental disability should be rationalized by the Inter-Agency Commission on children's rights recommended by the UN Committee on the Rights of the Child. There should be a role for the Ministry of Education at every stage of the child's development, to devise an education program in line with Article 2 of Protocol No. 1 to the ECHR.
- The Ministry of Justice should take full operational responsibility for the administration of the penitentiary system, using its own staff to prevent and contain disorders whenever they might arise. These staff should be specially trained in using non-violent techniques where possible, and in assessing the risk posed by prisoners on an individual basis.
- The relationship between the Ministry of Justice and Ministry of Internal Affairs should be clarified. Special police units that do not have the appropriate training should not be used to maintain order within the prison system, nor should prisoners be used to maintain discipline.
- The Ministry of Justice should review its policy towards life sentence prisoners and propose amendments to existing legislation to ensure it is brought into conformity with international standards for the treatment of long-term prisoners and the recommendations of the CPT.
- Solitary confinement as a standard form of punishment should be abolished. If solitary confinement is applied it should be imposed on a case-by-case basis for short and clearly defined periods, under close medical supervision. Special forms of restraint on prisoners, such as handcuffs, should be used only in conformity with international standards.
- Prisoners serving life sentences should have opportunities for the periodic review of their sentences by a court, in adversarial proceedings and with their own participation.

- The Russian Federation authorities should initiate a systematic judicial review of all life sentences passed before the new Criminal Procedure Code was adopted in December 2001.

On combating human rights violations in the Chechen Republic

The Russian Federation should take effective measures without delay to end the climate of impunity in the Chechen Republic, including through:

- Holding comprehensive and impartial investigations into allegations of violations of international human rights and humanitarian law, including war crimes, committed in the Chechen Republic, and bringing those responsible to justice in accordance with international standards.
- Allowing the Organization for Security and Co-operation in Europe (OSCE) to reopen a mission in Chechnya, with the power to exercise the full mandate laid down in the Decision of the Permanent Council in April 1995, including in relation to human rights.
- Extending invitations to the UN Special Rapporteurs on torture and on extrajudicial, summary or arbitrary executions, and granting unrestricted access to Chechnya to independent media and human rights monitors, including from international organizations.

Appendix: Articles 5 and 6 of the European Convention on Human Rights

Article 5

1. Everyone has the right to liberty and security of person. No one shall be deprived of his liberty save in the following cases and in accordance with a procedure prescribed by law:
    a) the lawful detention of a person after conviction by a competent court;
    b) the lawful arrest or detention of a person for non-compliance with the lawful order of a court or in order to secure the fulfilment of any obligation prescribed by law;
    c) the lawful arrest or detention of a person effected for the purpose of bringing him before the competent legal authority on reasonable suspicion of having committed an offence or when it is reasonably considered necessary to prevent his committing an offence or fleeing after having done so;
    d) the detention of a minor by lawful order for the purpose of educational supervision or his lawful detention for the purpose of bringing him before the competent legal authority;
    e) the lawful detention of persons for the prevention of the spreading of infectious diseases, of persons of unsound mind, alcoholics or drug addicts or vagrants;
    f) the lawful arrest or detention of a person to prevent his effecting an unauthorised entry into the country or of a person against whom action is being taken with a view to deportation or extradition.
2. Everyone who is arrested shall be informed promptly, in a language which he understands, of the reasons for his arrest and of any charge against him.

3. Everyone arrested or detained in accordance with the provisions of paragraph 1(c) of this article shall be brought promptly before a judge or other officer authorised by law to exercise judicial power and shall be entitled to trial within a reasonable time or to release pending trial. Release may be conditioned by guarantees to appear for trial.

4. Everyone who is deprived of his liberty by arrest or detention shall be entitled to take proceedings by which the lawfulness of his detention shall be decided speedily by a court and his release ordered if the detention is not lawful.

5. Everyone who has been the victim of arrest or detention in contravention of the provisions of this article shall have an enforceable right to compensation.

Article 6

1. In the determination of his civil rights and obligations or of any criminal charge against him, everyone is entitled to a fair and public hearing within a reasonable time by an independent and impartial tribunal established by law. Judgment shall be pronounced publicly but the press and public may be excluded from all or part of the trial in the interests of morals, public order or national security in a democratic society, where the interests of juveniles or the protection of the private life of the parties so require, or to the extent strictly necessary in the opinion of the court in special circumstances where publicity would prejudice the interests of justice.

2. Everyone charged with a criminal offence shall be presumed innocent until proved guilty according to law.

3. Everyone charged with a criminal offence has the following minimum rights:

    a) to be informed promptly, in a language which he understands and in detail, of the nature and cause of the accusation against him;

    b) to have adequate time and facilities for the preparation of his defence;

    c) to defend himself in person or through legal assistance of his own choosing or, if he has not sufficient means to

pay for legal assistance, to be given it free when the
interests of justice so require;

d) to examine or have examined witnesses against him and
to obtain the attendance and examination of witnesses
on his behalf under the same conditions as witnesses
against him;

e) to have the free assistance of an interpreter if he
cannot understand or speak the language used in court.

Endnotes

1 This report is based on many diverse sources, including written testimony of victims; reports from local human rights non-governmental organizations (NGOs) and ombudsmen; features in the regional and electronic press; legal texts, court judgments, parliamentary questions and government reports; and statements by the international community. It also draws heavily on firsthand material collected on field trips, and especially on trial observations; interviews with judges, members of parliament and regional ombudsmen; work with local human rights NGOs and on-site interviews with the victims of human rights violations.

2 The Russian Federation is divided into 89 Subjects – 49 regions (*oblasts*), 21 republics, 10 autonomous districts (*okrugs*), six territories (*krais*), two federal cities and one autonomous region (*oblast*).

3 V. Terebilov, "*Perestroika* demands legal reform", Moscow, Novosti 1988, cites these figures as of 1 November 1988.

4 See, for instance, the 1980 Amnesty International report on the USSR, *Prisoners of Conscience: Their Treatment and Conditions* (AI Index: EUR 46/004/1980) as well as other thematic reports on the imprisonment of Helsinki monitors; the imprisonment of dissenting Baptists; the punishment of free trade unionists; and the use of false criminal charges against dissenters.

5 The four Constitutions were promulgated in 1918, 1924, 1936 and 1977.

6 For further detailed information on the *propiska*, see Amnesty International's report *'Dokumenty!': Discrimination on grounds of race in the Russian Federation* (AI Index: EUR 46/001/2003).

7 In October 1993 the parliament was besieged and shelled by government troops, then dissolved, after persistently voting against President Yeltsin's legislative bills.

8 The Russian Federation has had two Constitutions, the first promulgated in 1991 when it became a sovereign state; the second in December 1993 after the forcible dissolution of the first sovereign parliament.

9 Thirteen people were sentenced to death under *Shari'a* law and publicly executed in the Chechen Republic in 1999, but an effective moratorium on death sentences has operated throughout the Russian Federation since then. Jury trials were to be introduced nationwide in January 2003 according to the new 2001 Criminal Procedure Code (CPC), but their introduction in Chechnya has since been delayed until 2007.

10 Article 15(4) of the 1993 Constitution of the Russian Federation.

11 Between 1995 and 2000 the Constitutional Court passed 19 rulings on criminal procedure, integrating specific standards of the European Convention on Human Rights (ECHR) into the Constitution. These were then necessarily included in the new CPC adopted in December 2001.

12 Ruling No. 7-P from 20 April 1999, on a query brought by Irkutsk City Court, Irkutsk Regional Court and the court of Sovetskii District in Nizhnii-Novgorod.

13 Article 34 of the ECHR states: "The Court may receive applications from any person, non-governmental organization or groups of individuals claiming to be the victim of a violation by one of the High Contracting Parties of the rights set forth in the Convention or the protocols thereto. The High Contracting Parties undertake not to hinder in any way the effective exercise of this right." Article 46 of the ECHR obliges a state party to abide by the final judgment of the Court in any case to which they are a party.

14 These concerned complaints about strikes, leaseholds on land, journalists' right of access to government information, and the violation of citizens' rights by executive bodies.

15 *Novie Izvestiia*, 18 July 2002.

16 Paradoxically both cases concerned combat duty done in 2001, at a time when President Putin had declared the military phase of the Chechnya war to be over. This point was not raised by either party in court, nor referred to by the judge in either case.

17 See the 1980 Amnesty International report, *Prisoners of Conscience in the USSR: Their Treatment and Conditions* (AI Index: EUR 46/004/1980), and *Human Rights in a Time of Change* (AI Index: EUR 46/022/1989), published in 1989.

18 Figures provided by Anatolii Pristavkin at a Conference on Clemency organized by the Russian Federation's Presidential Administration and the Council of Europe in Velikii Novgorod on 25-26 October 2000.

19 His report, *Report of the Activity of the Federal Human Rights Commissioner of the Russian Federation for the year 2000*, is available in Russian on www.ombudsman.gov.ru.

20 They are in the following Subjects: Altai; Amur; Arkhangelsk; Astrakhan; Bashkortostan; Ingushetia; Kaliningrad; Kalmykia; Kemerovo; Komi; Krasnodar; Krasnoiarsk; Lipetsk; Moscow Region; Perm; Samara; Saratov; Smolensk; Stavropol; Sverdlovsk; Tatarstan; Volgograd and Yakutia (Sakha).

21 See, for instance, the 2000 report of the Ombudsman of Astrakhan Region, listing 132 decrees of the regional administration that were unconstitutional and invalid because they had never been published. The decrees, however, were not suspended following the Ombudsman's report.

22 The so-called "anti-Zionist committees" of the Brezhnev era constituted one such example and the human rights commission of Fedor Burlatskii, in the Gorbachev era, another. Anti-Zionist Committees appeared briefly in major cities in the late 1970s, ostensibly set up by members of the public and often including prominent Jewish academics or military servicemen. They criticized Israeli and US policies in the Middle East at the height of the Cold War, and vanished in the Gorbachev era. The Burlatskii Human Rights Commission, consisting of prominent Moscow lawyers, was set up in 1988 to receive individual human rights complaints and to mediate between the USSR and human rights groups abroad. It issued the first invitation to Amnesty International to speak with the Soviet authorities.

23 Amnesty International has expressed concern at the ineffectiveness of these investigations and the lack of prosecutions. See, for example, *The Russian Federation: Denial of justice* (AI Index: EUR 46/027/2002).

24 According to a study published by the Moscow-based thinktank INDEM in May 2002, these unlawful killings would be impossible without the acquiescence of law enforcement agencies protecting people from the worlds of finance and political power, and thereby creating networks of corruption. The procuracy and the traffic police are the chief culprits, INDEM alleges, and their clients come mostly from political parties across the spectrum. Amnesty International is not in a position to confirm or refute such allegations.

25 Resolution 2001/24 of the UN Commission on Human Rights, UN Doc: E/CN.4/Res/2001/24. The resolution strongly condemned the continued use of disproportionate and indiscriminate force by Russian federal military forces, federal service and state agents, including attacks against civilians, and serious violations of human rights and humanitarian law, including "disappearances", extrajudicial executions, torture and other inhuman and degrading treatment in the Chechen Republic. It also strongly condemned "terrorist activities and attacks" and breaches of international humanitarian law perpetrated by Chechen fighters. It called on the parties to take immediate steps to stop the ongoing fighting and indiscriminate use of force, and to seek as a matter of urgency a political solution which fully respects the sovereignty and territorial integrity of the Russian Federation. It called on the authorities to establish a national broad-based and independent commission of inquiry to investigate promptly allegations of violations of human rights and humanitarian law to establish the truth and identify those responsible with a view to bringing them to justice and preventing impunity. It reiterated

requests made in 2000 to facilitate visits by the UN Special Rapporteurs on torture and on extrajudicial, summary or arbitrary executions, and the Special Representative of the UN Secretary-General for Internally Displaced Persons.

26 These are set down in Opinion 193 (1996) of the Parliamentary Assembly of the Council of Europe, EOPIN193.WP 1403, available on the Parliamentary Assembly website from the general portal, www.coe.int.

27 The reservations relate to Articles 5(3) and (4) of the ECHR on the obligation to ensure a person arrested or detained on a criminal charge is brought promptly before a judge and tried within a reasonable time or released pending trial, and the obligation to ensure that every person who is deprived of their liberty is entitled to take proceedings before a court which will speedily determine the legality of the detention and order release if the detention is not lawful.

28 Reported in *ITAR-TASS*.

29 AI Index: EUR 46/027/2002.

30 Public Statement on the Russian Federation, 10 July 2001, CPT/Info (2001) 15.

31 Quoted in *Interfax* on 6 March 2003.

32 See *Russian Federation: Justice must be done* (AI Index: EUR 46/030/2003).

33 Under Articles 2, 3, 13 and Article 1 of Protocol 1 to the ECHR respectively.

34 Under Article 1 of Protocol 1 to the ECHR, and Article 6 respectively.

35 Under Articles 3, 6, and 5(3) of the ECHR respectively.

36 Under Article 6(1) of the ECHR.

37 UN Doc: CCPR/C/69/D/770/1997.

38 Quoted in Opinion No. 193 (1996) on Russia's request for membership of the Council of Europe. Assembly debate on 25 January 1996 (6th and 7th sittings). See Doc. 7443, report of the Political Affairs Committee and Doc. 7463, opinion of the Committee on Legal Affairs and Human Rights. Text adopted by the Assembly on 25 January 1996. OPIN193 (1996).

39 Ibid.

40 AI Index: EUR 46/021/2002.

41 See Amnesty International, *UN Commission on Human Rights: Defeat of Chechnya resolution extremely disappointing* (AI Index: EUR 46/033/2003).

42 In Resolution 1323 available through the Council of Europe portal www.coe.int.

43 See the case law section of the website of the European Court of Human Rights on www.echr.coe.int.

44 One was brought by Denmark against Turkey for alleged ill-treatment of a Danish detainee in 1996, and the other was brought by Cyprus against Turkey, regarding the consequences of Turkish military operations in Northern Cyprus in 1974.

45 Recommendation 1600 (2003), adopted on 2 April 2003.

46 *"Pravo i Sila"*, *Moskovskii komsomolets*, 18 May 1991, cited in "Executive Power and Soviet Politics" ed. Eugene Huskey, New York, 1992.

47 See the Russian Ministry of Justice website: www.minjust.ru, Archive Section.

48 See, for instance, *Torture in Russia: This Man-Made Hell* (AI Index: EUR 46/004/1997).

49 In 1998 the administration of the penitentiary system was transferred to the Ministry of Justice as one of the commitments the Russian Federation undertook on joining the Council of Europe.

50 See, most recently, the 2002 Amnesty International report, *The Russian Federation: Denial of Justice* (AI Index: EUR 46/027/2002).

51 This is in spite of the state's obligations under Article 9(4) of the ICCPR to ensure that anyone deprived of their liberty has access to a court to determine the legality of their detention, or to order their release if the detention is unlawful.

52 Professor A.S. Gorelik, Dr A.D. Nazarov and Dr N.G. Stoyko, "The fairness of judicial hearings and the provision of a right to defence in criminal justice" ("*Spravedlivost sudebnogo razbiratelstva i obespechenie prava na zashchitu v ugolovnom sudoproizvodstve*"), Krasnoiarsk 2000.

53 These circumstances are the following: a) when the deprivation of freedom is legal and follows the judgment of a competent court; b) when an individual has failed to carry out the lawful judgments of a court, or to ensure that s/he carries out another obligation prescribed by law; c) to bring someone to trial on well-founded suspicion that s/he has broken the law, or is about to do so, or to prevent him or her hiding after committing it; d) to provide supervision of a juvenile, in accordance with a legal decision or to bring a juvenile before a competent organ; e) lawful detention of individuals to prevent them spreading infectious diseases, or of the mentally ill, alcoholics, drug addicts and beggars.

54 According to publicly available information from the Registry of the European Court of Human Rights, via www.coe.int.

55 This was set down in the Law of Implementation of the Criminal Procedure Code of the Russian Federation , dated 18 December 2001, No. 177-F3.

56 The ruling concerned complaints brought by three former detainees: S. Malenkin, R. Martynov and S. Pustovalov. For the full text in Russian, see www.ks.rfnet.ru.

57 In other rulings it found that the *propiska* system illegally restricted the electoral rights of people in North Ossetia-Alania (November 1995); and illegally prevented people from concluding property contracts in Krasnodar Territory (October 1998). In October 1991 the USSR Committee of Constitutional Supervision had also ruled that the *propiska* violated the right to freedom of movement.

58 See *A Commentary to the Constitution*, ed. V.A. Chetverin, Moscow 1997, p168, footnote 48.

59 Ruling of 4 April 1996, No. 9-P.

60 AI Index: EUR/46/001/2003.

61 The governments of the Republics of Sakha (Yakutia) in eastern Siberia, and Adygey in the south of the Russian Federation challenged the basis of this law, but its constitutionality was upheld by the Constitutional Court on 12 April 2002 in Ruling No. 8-P.

62 Article 29 of the law On the General Principles for Organizing Legislative (Representative) and Executive Organs of State power for the Subjects of the Federation.

63 Ibid Article 29-1 (2).

64 Ibid Article 29-1 (3).

65 Ibid Article 29-1 (6).

66 According to Article 3 of the law "On the general principles for organizing legislative (representative) and executive organs of state power in the Subjects of the Federation".

67 Under Article 15(4) of the Constitution, international standards prevail in cases of discrepancy.

68 The authorities have shown a contradictory attitude towards immigration. The Ministry of Internal Affairs, which is responsible for the Federal Migration Service, frequently spoke out in 2002 in favour of restricting the influx of migrant workers and taxing people who employ them. The Academy of Sciences' Institute of National Economic Forecasting, however, took the opposite view. Its Director, Zhanna Zaenchkovskaia, told the newspaper *Kommersant* on 25 April 2002 that tightening immigration policy ran counter to good sense and economic reality.

69 *Rossisskaia gazeta*, 31 July 2002.

70 AI Index: EUR 46/001/2003.

71 Amnesty International issued press releases on this. See, for example, AI Index: EUR 46/047/1999.

72 This case is reported in detail in a submission by Human Rights Watch to the (UN) Committee on the Elimination of Racial Discrimination on the occasion of the Committee's review of the Russian Federation's 17th periodic report, 24 February 2003. The whole submission is available on www.hrw.org.

73 Quoted in the newspaper *MK*, 30 October 2002.

74 According to complaints received from Chechens in Moscow by State *Duma* deputy Aslambek Aslakhanov between 28 October 2002 and 9 February 2003.

75 Different sources produce different numbers for the total of hostages taken. A figure of 979 is given by some, based on the list of individual names and outcomes compiled on the website www.grani.ru on 28 November 2002. The figures given by the Russian Federation Labour and Social Security Ministry on 6 November 2002 in the newspaper *Nezavisimaia gazeta* are lower. They claim that 858 hostages had been taken: 121 lower than the www.grani-ru figure.

76 According to the website www.grani.ru, the Major General survived the siege but his daughter was killed by the gas which the authorities used to end the siege.

77 Quoted in www.newsru.com on 27 October 2002.

78 The Russian Federation Ministry of Health said in mid-December that 129 hostages had died. For the same date, www.grani.ru documented the deaths of 139 people, and said that a further 68 – whom it named – remained unaccounted for.

79 See Amnesty International's report, *Concerns in Europe and Central Asia,* July-December 2002 (AI Index: EUR 01/002/2003).

80 Instruction of the Mayor of Moscow of 24 January 2003, on the website www.mos.ru.

81 The Belgian toxicologist and UN expert on war crimes in Kosovo, Professor A. Heyndrickx, identified the substance as a mixture of fentanyl and the toxic compound BZ, in a conversation with staff of the US-based Jamestown Foundation on 4 November 2002. Quoted in: www.chechnya.jamestown.org.

82 In January 2003 it was reported that nine Ukrainian hostages were planning to sue the Russian federal authorities for material and moral damages, but Amnesty International does not know if they have done so.

83 Amnesty International was asked not to identify the facility in case the local non-governmental organization which facilitated the visit would be denied access in the future.

84 Data from the draft third report of the Russian Federation to the Committee on the Rights of the Child.

85 Instruction of the Ministry of Health of the USSR "On Medical Indicators and Contra-Indicators for Placements in *Internats*" of 5-7 September 1978, No. 14/12/2495 MK.

86 Available in Russian on his website: www.ombudsman.gov.ru.

87 UN Doc: CRC/C/15/Add.110, of 10 November 1999.

88 For example, the laws On Pensions and Disability Allowance; On War Invalids; and On Social Services for Elderly Invalids.

89 Russian Federation Government Ruling No. 288 of 12 March 1997: "On confirming the Standard for Special (Corrective) training establishments for the education of trainees with mental disabilities", supplemented by Government Ruling No. 212 of 10 March 2000 "On Amendments to the Standard for Special (Corrective) training establishments for the education of trainees with mental disabilities".

90 Consideration of Reports Submitted by States Parties under Article 44 of the Convention on the Rights of the Child, Addendum: Russian Federation, CRC/C/65/Add.5, para. 236.

91 Consideration of Reports Submitted by States Parties under Article 144 of the Convention on the Rights of the Child, Addendum: Russian Federation, CRC/C/15/Add.4, Table 14. In the later report, the Russian Federation said it had improved detection of child abuse and taken proportionally more children into state care.

92 These are all directives, pre-dating the formation of the Russian Federation, of the Ministry of Social Welfare: No. 52 of 25 April 1962: "On official norms for medical and educational personnel in homes for mentally retarded children"; Instruction No. 35 of 6 April 1979 confirming a provision "On children's homes and *internats* (orphanages) for mentally retarded children"; and Directive No. 132 of 22 October 1986 "On standard structures and staffing for institutions within the Ministry of Social Welfare of the RSFSR".

93 Ministry of Social Welfare Order No. 132 of 22 October 1986 "On typical structures and typical conditions in institutions in the system of the Ministry of Social Welfare of the RFSFR".

94 "Standard job specifications for workers in educational institutions of the Russian Federation", No. 463/1268 of 31 August 1995 and Decree No. 46 of the Ministry of Labour and the State Higher Education Commitee, dated 17 August 1995.

95 Report produced by the Ministry of Labour, page 26.

96 Ibid, page 47.

97 Fifteen federal and 21 regional regulations on disability are listed in the report.

98 Vestnik No. 2(3) 2002 of the Plenipotenitary for Human Rights in Moscow Region www.ombudsmanmo.ru.

99 Para 6 of the Concluding Observations of the Committee on the Rights of the Child; Russian Federation 18/02/93, UN Doc: CRC/C/15/Add 4.

100 Ibid, para 17.

101 Concluding Observations of the Committee on the Rights of the Child: Russian Federation 10/11/99, UN Doc: CRC/C/15/ Add 110, para 36.

102 Ibid, para 39.

103 Ibid, para 40.

104 These possibilities are provided in Article 12 (4) of the Punishment-Implementation Code.

105 *Otriad militsii osobogo naznacheniia.*

106 They were charged under Articles 286(3), 208, 209 and 5 of the Criminal Code.

107 This is the explanation given by the Ozhegov etymological dictionary of the Russian language.

108 For details of the submission, see Application No. 47095/99 by Valerii Yermilovich Kalashnikov against Russia on the website of the European Court of Human Rights, www.echr.coe.int.

109 According to Article 57(1) of the Criminal Code.

110 Article 105, Article 277, Article 295, Article 317 and Article 357 respectively.

111 Articles 80(2) and 126 of the Punishment-Implementation Code.

112 Substantive Statement dated 10 July 2001, CPT/Inf(2001) 15. Available from the CPT website via the general Council of Europe portal: www.coe.int.

113 Article 118(3) of the Punishment-Implementation Code.

114 Article 112(6) of the Punishment-Implementation Code.

115 Article 127(6) of the Punishment-Implementation Code.

116 Information from Anatolii Pristavkin, Presidential Adviser on clemency issues, February 2003. On 3 March 2003 the Ministry of Justice website reported that eight new special regime colonies had opened and 14 additional "special regime" units had been built in existing colonies, but did not say where. See www.minjust.ru.

117 See press releases on www.minjust.ru from 17 and 18 December 2002.

118 Article 50(3) of the Constitution. In 2001 the Ministry of Justice sent a letter to the Directors of corrective labour institutions, advising them to forward clemency petitions only from prisoners who had already served two thirds of their sentence. A copy of this letter is in the possession of Amnesty International. It is unclear when a prisoner with a life sentence, therefore, will be eligible to petition for clemency.

119 Article 3 is On the Prohibition of Torture.

120 *Hussain v the UK*, 21 February 1996, REF 00000561, available on www.echr.coe.int.

121 According to Article 175(9) of the Punishment-Implementation Code. The Code does not state what the statutory part of the punishment is for life sentence prisoners, or other categories of prisoner. This information may possibly be contained in administrative regulations of the Ministry of Justice.

122 Article 176(1) of the Punishment-Implementation Code.

123 Article 176(3) of the Punishment-Implementation Code

124 Materials from a Clemency Conference in November 2002 held between the Russian Federation Presidential Administration and the Council of Europe in Odintsovskii district, Moscow Region.

125 They were established after President Putin's decree of 28 December 2001, disbanding the federal clemency commission.

126 See Chapter 3 of this report, which describes changes to the Criminal Procedure Code.